SPIRITUAL
Lovemaking

About the Authors

Jody Baron is an independent researcher and writer. She has written over a dozen books as a ghostwriter of spiritual and New Age material, including Tantric sex. She is the founding moderator of The Abe Forum, an active online discussion of the Law of Attraction.

Peter Beamish is a television producer with over twenty-five years of experience, including in-depth interviews with Neale Donald Walsch (*Conversations with God*) and Esther and Jerry Hicks (*Introducing Abraham: The Secret Behind the Secret*).

Please visit Jody and Peter at
www.spirituallovemaking.com

SPIRITUAL
Lovemaking
Relax into Sex & Awaken into Life

JODY BARON
and PETER BEAMISH

Llewellyn Publications
Woodbury, Minnesota

First Edition
First Printing, 2013

Cover image and part page image © Iakov Kalinin/Bigstock.com
Cover design by Adrienne Zimiga
Editing by Andrea Neff

Llewellyn Publications is a registered trademark of Llewellyn Worldwide Ltd.

Library of Congress Cataloging-in-Publication Data
Baron, Jody, 1953–
   Spiritual lovemaking : relax into sex & awaken into life / by Jody Baron and Peter Beamish. — 1st ed.
      p. cm.
   Includes index.
   ISBN 978-0-7387-3431-6
1. Sex instruction. 2. Man-woman relationships. I. Beamish, Peter, 1957–
II. Title.
   HQ64.B365 2013
   613.9071—dc23
                          2012028481

Llewellyn Worldwide Ltd. does not participate in, endorse, or have any authority or responsibility concerning private business transactions between our authors and the public.
   All mail addressed to the author is forwarded but the publisher cannot, unless specifically instructed by the author, give out an address or phone number.
   Any Internet references contained in this work are current at publication time, but the publisher cannot guarantee that a specific location will continue to be maintained. Please refer to the publisher's website for links to authors' websites and other sources.

Llewellyn Publications
A Division of Llewellyn Worldwide Ltd.
2143 Wooddale Drive
Woodbury, MN 55125-2989
www.llewellyn.com

Printed in the United States of America

Dedicated to
John Conrad Tiemann,
of blessed memory.
You set the bar for strong, gentle, and loving.

Tuned in. Tapped in. Turned on…

—ABRAHAM-HICKS

… Times two.

Contents

Appreciation

To Peter—my precious best friend—my deepest thanks for your vision and inspiration. Thank you for living life with an enthusiasm that sees sparks in my ideas and then fans them into flames of manifestation. Thank you for noticing things! Thank you for being a keen observer and for constantly pointing out the amazing and the beautiful. You have my unending appreciation for your creativity, your insight, your humor, and your love, and for showing them to me every day. Thank you for being part of my soul on this and so many other exciting journeys. We're having so much fun!

To Jody—my rock, my guide. When you and I joined forces—living, traveling, and loving together—everything, including our creative projects, took on an amazing vibrancy. That's how this book was born! You are the most powerful creator that I know. And, may I say, you are *a really good writer!* Thank you for being by my side through joy after joy, and bliss after bliss.

Peter and I most affectionately acknowledge Abraham (www.Abraham-Hicks.com) and Esther and Jerry Hicks for leading us back to the knowledge that "life is *supposed* to be fun!" We have woven the spirit of their message into this book, just as it is woven into our lives. Thank you from the bottom of our hearts for teaching us to "let go of the oars" and float downstream to the life of our dreams. Jerry Hicks made his transition to non-physical during the preparation of this manuscript. I think of him often, and when inspiration flags, I call forth his wonderful musical laughter. Hearing that in my mind never fails to put the writing back on track!

Thank you, Neale Donald Walsch (www.NealeDonald Walsch.com), for looking me squarely in the eye and saying, "Your next book will be in your own voice." Your assurance allowed me to assure myself and to stop using my ability and insights only to ghostwrite others' material. You guided me to remain open for a message I wanted to deliver myself. We both knew it would be about spirituality, but ... I never would have guessed that it would also be about sex!

Diana Richardson (www.loveforcouples.com), thank you for your deep knowledge of and abiding love for the ancient *tantras*. Your books, your years of experience with couples, and your research are what made this lighthearted guide to relaxed sex possible. Your spirit shines through this work, and you are deeply appreciated.

Richard Franklin Morse, your song "I Love My Life" has become the theme song for our lives. We've done our best to weave its feeling through the words in this book. Thank you for your creation.

Every moment unfolds before my eyes
with infinite sweet surprise.
I love my life.
And with every breath that comes and goes,
abundant blessing overflows.
I love my life. I love my life.

And to the rest of you—oh, so very many of you—you know who you are. Feel the love! We feel abundantly blessed to share the journey through this life with you. In fact, every day, Peter and I feel our hearts have so expanded in appreciation of so very many amazing souls—our friends, our children, and a whole world of others who have blessed our path—that we could write another whole book just singing your praises! Maybe we'll do that someday. Meanwhile, we offer you each the words in this volume, and hope you'll consider this our sincere gift of love. All of your contributions, your love and support, your laughter and your wisdom, are so very warmly acknowledged.

INTRODUCTION

Who Are Jody and Peter and Why Relax into Sex?

We teach what we most need to learn.

A wise person once pointed out that the best teachers are not those who have mastered what they are trying to convey, but those who are striving to master it. As counterintuitive as this may sound, Peter and I have found it to be true in our own lives, as it's been true for our most influential teachers.

We are not therapists, doctors, life coaches, or healers.

We *are* two people who have figured it out. We have been blessed to have discovered how to truly relax into the present moment, and we reap the benefits of this knowledge every day. Peter and I have walked spiritual and sexual journeys from the most mundane and prosaic to the most joyful and fulfilling on every level. This book will show you how easy it will be for you to do the same.

Before discovering and using the information you'll find in this book, Peter and I would have told you we thought sex was great. With hindsight, we realize we were experiencing some very common limitations, all of which changed when we entered the world of spiritual sex. While of course we continue to deepen our understanding on a continual basis, we've come to a place where we are bursting with what we've figured out so far about the relationship between our sexual lives and the rest of life, and how spirituality plays across the board. We feel so enlivened and enriched by relaxed, spiritual lovemaking, and all that flows from it into the rest of our lives, that we want to share it with everyone who attracts our material into their experience.

We've had a lot of help on the path to this understanding and knowledge, and we have accepted and followed inspiration as it has come, often from the most unexpected of sources. We've been privileged to personally know and learn from some of today's most gifted spiritual teachers. At their feet, so to speak, we've honed our knowledge of the truths of how things work, and we have lived the teachings with regard to lovemaking and every other aspect of our lives. And we continue to live them, day in and day out, with more amazing results than we ever could have envisioned.

I've been a writer for many years, and over a dozen books have been published with me as ghostwriter and/or researcher. This was fine, because I loved to write but did not feel my own book bubbling within me. I did not have a story of my own that I felt passionate about telling. Until now.

A few years before I began to write this book, I had an opportunity to have several long and personal conversations with Neale Donald Walsch, author of *Conversations with God*. Neale is one of the most widely read spiritual authors and guides of our time. When he pointedly told me that I was destined to begin to write my own message, in my own voice, I took what he said and held it close to my heart, waiting.

Nobody was more surprised than I was to discover that my own voice would be telling people about a better way to have sex!

A few years before my meeting with Neale, I was given an assignment by a publisher to write a book about Tantric sex. The *tantras* are ancient Hindu mystical texts that describe many of the basic precepts of the body-mind connection, and explain how to make the various aspects of human life transcend the physical and become spiritual activities. I learned that, while this knowledge has been around for thousands of years, it holds universal truths for our time, as for all time. I thoroughly researched the subject of Tantric sex and completed the writing.

That book was published, and I moved on to other projects, never having been truly moved by the information I had studied so thoroughly. I had never really internalized the material about which I had just handed in a well-written and praised manuscript. I had not made a true connection between those ancient teachings and our own real and present and expanding lives today.

Although I now considered myself an "expert" in the teachings of Tantric sex by virtue of my research and having communicated the ideas in that book, I had no real sense at that time what the *essence* of spiritual sex could and would do to open up not just my sex life but every aspect of my being. My personal journey of spiritual understanding was only in its infancy then, and I did not realize at the time that I'd just laid an important brick in the foundation of my new and expanded life.

Soon afterward, my dad made his transition to non-physical, and his absence from this life spurred my spiritual journey in earnest. I was certain that somewhere there was a "secret" to the way things really work in the universe. I was led to the teachings of Abraham-Hicks and other spiritual teachers, and I drank in the concept that I create my own reality, and that everything is made up of energy that we control with our thoughts and emotions. I studied the message of the importance of alignment between our physical and non-physical selves, and how all negative emotions and missteps in our physical existence stem from a misalignment of our lives with our inner beings. Experiencing many "aha!" moments along the way, I joyfully continued to expand my knowledge and understanding of these concepts.

Peter and I were "awakening" in parallel. We were born in similar northern cities, had similar backgrounds, and had been instilled with similar family values. After marrying (twice each) and raising children (three each), with several academic degrees between us and numerous career adventures—all of which were wonderful relationships and experiences we would not trade for the world—we met in midlife having each come to similar crossroads where we wondered: What's next? What more is in store?

Peter:

I was taught about sex—and life—in much the same way that most of us were probably taught: through my parents, family, friends, school, and the media. I was busy jumping through hoops trying to please people and spent very little time thinking about how life might really work. I was in my forties by the time my searching led me to the answers, and my spiritual asking brought me to the feet of some of the most profound teachers of our time. The idea that life is actually supposed to be fun? That we are all part of one universal energy? The knowledge that by following our bliss, we'll actually end up where we want to go? This was all sweet music to my ears.

I, too, studied the teachings of Abraham-Hicks, and my favorite concept of all was that of "letting go of the oars"—knowing it's not only okay, but actually in my best interest, to let go of the oars of life, letting life itself take me where I want to go. I discovered I could stop striving and start "being," and actually achieve far more and in a more interesting and delightful way than I ever could have dreamed.

When we met, Peter and I both had already spent years internalizing the messages of many of the same spiritual teachers of today. I, too, was finding that to "drop the oars" and *allow* myself to flow easily to the life of my dreams was pivotal for my spiritual growth and understanding. This phrase essentially means *relaxing* and allowing the universe to work its magic for you, rather than making constant effort and plans. This simple change of assumption about what makes life tick led to profound change for each of us. And the change was rapid. We each experienced relationships shifting and ending, and dreams formed and realized.

We remained fascinated by and immersed in the spiritual teachings as we continued to hone our understanding.

Peter Talks about Our Early Relationship:
When Jody and I met, what began as a friendship between kindred spirits soon became so close a bond that we were finishing each other's sentences and reading each other's minds. We talked, talked, talked our way through years of a wild-ride life that included many spiritual aha's along with plenty of ups and downs of all kinds. As we became closer, and as our sexual relationship bonded us and expanded our tie, the subject of our many-hours-per-day ramblings was, more often than not, relationships. We called it "Relationships 101."

In 2008 a friend gifted Peter with Diana Richardson's book *The Heart of Tantric Sex.* It was exactly the right book at the right time. Spiritual lovemaking felt like the next logical step to Peter, and he read the book several times, each time becoming more inspired and uplifted. Over a period of several years, Peter and I traveled thousands of miles on a series of glorious road trips we dubbed the "Amplified Stardust Tours." As we made our way through the mountains, deserts, beaches, and forests of North America, Peter often expressed his appreciation for and excitement about the ancient yet universal and timeless ideas you are about to explore in this book. He knew intuitively that this material had the ability to transform us, physically and spiritually.

We practiced spiritual lovemaking and slowly broadened our understanding of it with plenty of joyous personal experience. What happened next is what planted the seed for this book to be born.

I realized that what I knew about Tantric (spiritual) sex and what I was learning in other areas of spirituality were actually all one lesson. Sex isn't just a metaphor for life; it's a vitally important part of life. And spiritual sex is completely different and oh so much more enriching and powerful than what we'd experienced previously.

Life ... sex ... it didn't matter. It all boiled down to one thing:

Relax!

I remember one particular afternoon, while shooting video at Big Sur, when Peter climbed with camera and tripod to an overhanging cliff and I looked out at the waves and pondered our ongoing "spiritual journey" and the unexpected discoveries we'd made along the way. I was beginning to understand how all of the thoughts and ideas I'd been attracting over the years had actually culminated in one deceptively simple and succinct message: *relax!* In fact, I believe that truly relaxing is the common theme in most spiritual teachings, when reduced to their essence. I have even come to understand that relaxing is the key to enjoying life as well as the answer to just about any complaint, discomfort, or dissatisfaction—physical or emotional—that we humans experience.

I was becoming more and more open to and fascinated with *relaxed spiritual sex.*

I opened myself up to nothing less than a whole new world. It was an awakening—a wondrous awakening. I felt a veil lifting. I felt I was being given something I'd been asking for on so many levels but just had not previously allowed to actualize. Relaxed spiritual sex had been waiting quietly in the wings while I tried all kinds of other sexual experiences (well, mostly the "traditional" kinds), and I didn't know what I was missing.

Many of us in this first part of the twenty-first century are shifting and growing as we search for knowledge. We sense that the way to feel more satisfied with life is to become more connected to our inner selves, and we want to be more authentic in the expression of our truths, but we aren't sure where to turn or what to change in our life circumstances, relationships, or behaviors to effect the shift.

My desire to become more authentically who-I-really-am led me on a delightful path and introduced me to so many amazing teachers and ideas. As I learned seemingly new and different concepts, I recognized that most of the truths felt familiar, as if I had always known them but had somehow temporarily forgotten them. I greeted each new revelation with a resonance deep within.

This same thing happened with spiritual lovemaking.

Relaxing into sex affords a most delightful way to know the self. It asks for presence, for openness, for acceptance, and therefore for authenticity. I hope, after reading this book, you'll agree that learning to really show up and be present for lovemaking carries its power far beyond the bedroom and has the capacity to revolutionize, in a gentle and natural way, your entire experience. When you are truly present for lovemaking, you become fully present for life.

You do not have to be on a "spiritual path" to benefit from spiritual sex. Even if you are the most down-to-earth, feet-on-the-ground person on the planet, somewhere inside you is that quiet knowing that you are "more" as well. Somewhere within you exists the knowledge that even when you are not *doing*—that is, when you are simply *being*—you are enough. You are strong, capable, and worthy. You have the natural inclination to be amazingly tuned in to all that is joyful and fulfilling in life. Relaxing into sex will put you in touch with the *more* that you always knew was attainable.

And what about your relationship? You will find that the relaxed you is capable of a close, abiding, and deep connection. Whatever the state of your partnership with your lover, and whatever efforts you have made before to come together with complete understanding and openness, when you relax into sex your connection will flow more easily and naturally than it ever could when trying to forge it out of effort, discussion, or analysis.

The ideas in this book have been around for thousands of years. Penned in ancient languages by the wisest of their time, the concepts of relaxed sex (or Tantric sex) have largely been forgotten by modern society. I hope this book will bring these ideas to you in a way that makes sense for the twenty-first century and shows how timelessly relevant spiritual lovemaking is and always will be. Your body and your spirit will remember! They will delight in being freed to experience the expansive joy that you are naturally capable of. Relaxed sex will inform the rest of your activities with grace, joy, and ease.

In this book I use the phrases "relaxed sex," "spiritual sex," and "Tantric sex" almost synonymously, since in reality they describe the same thing: conscious, present lovemaking. Some of the concepts offered may seem self-explanatory and even obvious at first reading, but I ask you to open yourself to seeing them in a light you haven't considered before: that of relaxation. The art of relaxing into sex will open you up to a whole new world. What may have seemed familiar will now take on a shimmer and a glow. Sometimes I'll present things in several different ways, revisiting points several times, hoping you will experience a number of aha moments, moments when you recognize what is truly different and new for you in relaxed sex.

Many couples say that after a time—for some it's weeks, for others it's many years—lovemaking loses much of its excitement. They may feel they've lost their sexual attraction to one another, even when love remains. If you are in a relationship filled with love and have a desire for more closeness, but you've lost your "chemistry," you'll find that what we offer here will restore your natural, free, exuberant desire. When you relax into sex and allow these ideas to take hold, you will experience renewed desire—true "electro-physical" attraction. And this new and stronger attraction knows no end. This isn't the novelty of a new sex toy, technique, or position. This is true connection. This is authentic expression of natural desire. Burnout or tiring of one another does not occur because the sex act is always new, free, fresh, and electrical.

Learning to relax and connect was the next step in the journey for me. I think it may be your next step as well. You are holding this book in your hands (or reading it on a screen) because your life has led you to this information. There are no coincidences, but only a flow of people, circumstances, and ideas, as you "ask" at each juncture in your life's journey. So I hope you'll relax into it and enjoy, accepting and allowing this simple knowledge into your life and using it to infuse you with its magic.

In this book, I take you into the heart of spiritual lovemaking and give you enough information to put it into practice immediately. As soon as you do, you will feel positive shifts.

You will change. There will be no turning back. The relaxed, present, authentic *you* will want to repeat the experience over and over, and each time it will be different than the last.

I don't want you to say, "What a nice idea," and then put this book on the shelf thinking you might try it someday. I want you to feel inspired to take your lover by the hand and ... *relax.*

Perhaps you are reading this on the train as you commute to work alone, or maybe you have lit a candle and you're reading it aloud to your lover in bed. Wherever you are, savor the words. Slow down and read slowly. Intend to allow a new feeling about lovemaking to take over. Maybe you haven't actually made love with your partner in years, or maybe you have sex every morning like clockwork. In any case, *relaxing* into it in the way you'll come to understand shortly is *new*, so have the intention to come to lovemaking in a new way, with a new mindset and a new curiosity for how this can work to transform you.

About the Exercises in This Book

Many of the most profound activities for grounding ourselves in the present moment and for practicing the principles of relaxing into sex are actually the simplest and easiest to perform. I hope that while you read this book you'll have a series of aha moments and feel renewed and inspired by the material, and resolve to bring these concepts into your lovemaking and your relationship. In fact, I'm so sure that you'll find value in the words here, in my own and Peter's experiences, and in the ancient knowledge of the Tantra, that I want to make certain I've given you every tool I know of in order to truly make use of that value.

When conceiving this book, Peter and I agreed it would not be a how-to manual. We personally do not really like being told what to do, and we assume you don't either. Instead, we decided to lay out the concepts, explain them fully, and otherwise essentially leave our readers to their own devices. However, when our publisher suggested that people may want more specific help in getting started, and after hearing feedback from many people who read the manuscript in its early form, we understood that in reality, sometimes being told how—in detail—and being given ideas on how to start in on something new, is wanted and expected. So after rethinking our approach, we delved into our own recent past and present use of this material and decided to offer readers some activities and exercises that will lead you gently into spiritual lovemaking and assure that the changes become ingrained in your behavior and inspire you onward.

Anything new, especially when it goes against the grain of habit, requires practice to really take hold. So don't give up. Take it a little at a time. You don't have to make love for ten hours the first time you decide to give spiritual lovemaking a try. There is a lifetime of lovemaking waiting for you, and each time can be different. Just resolve to take something, however small, from relaxed sex and try it each time, and soon you'll be seeing expansion far beyond your wildest expectations, both in the bedroom and beyond.

So here we go.

PART ONE

The Basics of Spiritual Sex

CHAPTER ONE

You Are Ready for Spiritual Sex

Sexual activity feeds the spirit.
—Diana Richardson

It's rather fashionable these days to be on a "spiritual jour-ney" of some kind. *Spirit* is a word that's used in a myriad of contexts, and it can have as many meanings as there are those who use it. So let's explain what is meant here when we say "the art of spiritual lovemaking."

What Is the Spirit?

The concepts of *spirit* and *spiritual* as we use them in this book haven't a thing to do with any religion or any kind of New Age or ritual practice.

Simply put, **the *spirit* is the non-physical part of the self.** You may have another term you prefer, such as *soul* or *inner being*. The words chosen don't matter, as long as we can agree that we each do have a part of the self that is not physical. If you are not sure you can subscribe to this belief, bear with me as I explain what I mean.

Each human being comes into this life with a physical body. That's obvious enough. The physical body can't be denied. It's present and accounted for. In fact, when we say "I" or "me," most of us are referring to the pile of bones and sinew we call our body.

But what about our emotions and mental faculties? Are these parts of the body? We seem to intuitively understand that a kind of duality is at work when we say things such as "my leg" or "I thought." In the first case, it seems the spirit owns the body, and in the second, it seems to mean the opposite. Let's agree that our feelings and thoughts can be called *non-physical*; that is, they cannot be pinpointed as part of our physical apparatus. And yet they are certainly integral parts of us. These aspects of our selves—those that can be thought of as separate from, though connected to and not entirely independent of, our physical bodies—make up the *spiritual,* or *non-physical,* aspects of our being.

In reality, the physical is part and parcel of the spiritual. We are all in fact spiritual beings having a physical experience through use of a physical body in this physical environment. For our purposes, however, we'll make the distinction between our physical bodies and our non-physical thoughts, feelings, and emotions.

Sometimes people say they are not interested in a relationship that is "just physical," or conversely they may say "our relationship is just for casual sex." However, in both cases this is not really possible. Since we are always made up of both our spiritual and physical aspects, one of these can never truly be absent. No matter how we characterize a relationship or an encounter, it is never "just" physical, because our spirit is always engaged.

When the physical and the non-physical aspects of our being are in alignment, we feel whole, relaxed, and at peace. When our physical experience is at odds with any of the aspects of our non-physical being, we may find ourselves oddly agitated, with a feeling of not "having it together" or of being "disconnected." When any kind of disharmony exists in the non-physical self (the thoughts and emotions), the physical body will also be in disharmony. The term *cognitive dissonance* in psychology is used to denote the disquiet one feels when actions are not in sync with thoughts and beliefs. We long to be in easy, authentic connection with our inner, non-physical being, our *spirit*. We feel discomfort, both physical and emotional, when we are not in alignment with our spirit, whether we use that term or call it something else.

It follows that disconnection from the non-physical, or spiritual, part of the self leads to an inability to fully connect with another person, either physically or spiritually. Clearly, a feeling of wholeness, a feeling that our body is in sync with our mind and heart, is a prerequisite to satisfying relationships of all kinds. Since connection with another person is not truly possible without aligning with the self first, the alignment of our physical and non-physical selves is paramount.

Aligning the Physical and Non-Physical Aspects of Your Being

A whole and aligned relationship with your inner, non-physical being allows the formation of an amazing connection with a partner. All of this can happen when you relax into sex. Relaxed, spiritual lovemaking will transform your relationship—not as a result of what your partner says or does, but because you will discover who you really are. You will allow yourself to be who you really are. You will find yourself in sync with yourself, and then with your partner, in deeper ways than you have ever experienced before.

Spiritual sex is lovemaking that helps bring about the alignment of the physical and non-physical aspects of our being. It is also the lovemaking that happens once we have achieved that alignment.

Ask yourself these questions:

• Do you ever wonder if you are a "good enough" lover? Do you feel it's your obligation to bring your partner to a peak of sexual excitement through your actions during sex?

• Do you sometimes feel too tired to want to bother making love with your partner?

• Do you ever feel that sex is a chore, or that it's something you are obligated to do?

- Has your physical attraction for your partner seemed to wane over the years, even though you love him or her as much as ever?
- Do you or your partner fall asleep right after love-making?
- Have you and your partner fallen into a habitual pattern of lovemaking? Does it sometimes feel like it's just the "same old same old"?
- Do you long for deep affection and connection but feel that sex has lost that aspect, or never had it to begin with?
- Do you or your partner sometimes use sex to relieve tension?

If you answered yes to even one of these questions, then this book has the potential to make a profound difference for you.

No matter what age you are, no matter how many sexual experiences or how many partners you've had, relaxing into sex is going to open up a whole new world of sweet surprise.

Imagine your ideal relationship with your partner. Close your eyes and go to a feeling of complete connection, of easy communication and understanding, and of giving and receiving love naturally and effortlessly. You don't even have to think about sex at first, if that doesn't come to mind immediately. For women especially, sex is often not among the first things they think of when imagining what it would be like to have the ideal, perfect, dreamy relationship with their spouse or lover.

Using the power of your imagination, play a little "movie" for yourself in your mind where you and your partner are enjoying the most intimate, stress-free, and enjoyable day ever. Whether you imagine the two of you skiing, lying on a beach, working on a project together, or just sitting on the couch, in your movie you and your partner are joyful and relaxed. Relaxed sex is actually going to help you move closer to this ideal—not by talking about what you want, but by cutting through and going directly to *taking* what you want: relaxed, intimate time with your lover, with nowhere to go and everything to feel. And it's going to be easy … as long as you allow it to be.

We've been misled. We've been taught that lovemaking comes as the culmination of an already close and intimate coupling. This misconception has robbed us of the magic that relaxed lovemaking can afford a relationship. We don't have to wait until things feel perfect to make love. Making love can be a vehicle to reaching the perfection we seek. "Plugging in," as Peter calls it, and making your bodies one physical unit *when you relax,* releases all of what is otherwise not working. Relaxed, goal-less physical union puts you right where you want to be. With bodies connected and minds willing, no possible way exists for either of you to do anything wrong. Your bodies intrinsically know what to do. They want to love; they want to be open and authentic. And they will be when you relax.

Relaxed sex does ask you to show up. That means that when you decide to try this, you make a commitment to yourself to see it through. You *decide* to make love in a spiritual manner and you *decide* to show up—vulnerable and trusting—no matter what else is going on in your relationship. Give yourself a chance to allow spiritual sex to perform its healing magic or to lift an already close and abiding connection to new and lofty heights.

Making Time for Lovemaking

Be aware that spiritual lovemaking takes time. True relaxation knows no deadlines and has no clocks.

I know. You have a life. You have places to go and things to do. Still, when you make lovemaking a priority and allow time for truly relaxing into sex, you'll emerge so energized and alive that everything else in your life will seem effortless and seem to take less time! The trade-off works in your favor in so many wonderful ways, so make time and take time for relaxing into sex.

Slow down. Imagine lovemaking that lasts for hours. Imagine coming together with your lover and not seeking the explosive release of orgasm, but rather experiencing an expansive orgasmic state! That is what relaxed sex will afford you. Rather than having an orgasm every time, you'll taste the delights of truly *being* orgasmic.

Make love for hours? Yes, you can. You will be shown how as you read on.

CHAPTER TWO

Sexual Energy

Most of us think we know what is meant by "sex" or "love-making." We know the mechanics of sexual intercourse. We know what goes where. We understand quite early on, even before our first actual sexual experience with a partner, that the sex act has a purpose and a goal called orgasm. We know orgasm feels good, and we want to feel as good as we possibly can as often as we can. Popular culture supports this.

Our pop literature dictates that the more orgasms we have, the better; and the more intense they are … well, better still. According to popular modern consensus, the ability to bring a partner to orgasm easily and quickly is what makes a man a good lover, and being more orgasmic is what makes a woman successful at the sex act. A profusion of manuals instruct us on what we should *do*, what actions to take (and sometimes even what words to say), so that sex with a partner will result in more and better orgasms.

If you have heard the term *sexual energy*, you may have thought of it as the "sex drive" or the "need for sexual release."

Well, get ready for a new idea!

The physical pleasure that transcends orgasm and the experience of deeply spiritual lovemaking can't be found through action-oriented, how-to instructions. It is not found by being "better" at goal-oriented sex.

Relaxing into sex will lead you to the realization that putting your focus on learning the how-tos of sex and on what you previously thought was entailed in "good" lovemaking has actually overshadowed the true wisdom of your body and robbed you (until now) of the absolute ecstasy that is available through the sex act.

What Is Sexual Energy?

This wisdom in your body is rooted in the concept of *sexual energy*. I know you've heard this term before, but I want to introduce you to a more accurate meaning of the phrase. Rarely do we think of our bodies as bioelectrical, energetic in a non-physical sense, or being surrounded by and acting upon an energy field. Yet this energy exists and is at work at all times. Sexual energy is part of the way things work, not just when we are making love but in our lives as a whole.

This omission from our modern sexual knowledge—our lack of awareness of our nature as energetic beings—has cut us off from an amazingly beautiful awareness of our full capabilities as sexual human beings. If we tune in and listen to our own inner guidance while letting go of goal-oriented action, we will discover a level of sexual enjoyment far beyond what the physical body is capable of experiencing by itself.

Sexual energy is the *life force* that flows through each and every one of us. Sexual energy is not limited to expression in sexual acts. It is part of our overall aliveness, our vital state, and it is with us always. This energy cannot be contained or denied. Sex is an extremely empowering force and goes far beyond immediate gratification or reproductive function. It is the power that feeds our entire life experience.

Channeling Sexual Energy

Sexual energy does not always drive toward orgasm. It is not the same as sexual excitement. Sexual energy can be channeled into actions that generate excitement, which is what most of us have become accustomed to. However, it can also be used to achieve ever deeper levels of feeling and a more profound sexual experience.

The sexual energy generated by our bodies runs through us along a path starting at the genitals, moving up to the brain, and circling back down and around again in an unending circuit. When the energy descends from the brain back to the genitals and we have built up sexual excitement through friction, fantasy, or other means, the urge to release the energy in orgasm is felt. If we have not employed friction, however, but rather have allowed the energy to travel without becoming excitement, release does not happen, and the energy is recirculated within the body, serving to revitalize us in profound ways. This is the way of relaxed sex. It does not mean we are to be sexually "frustrated." Rather, it means we learn to observe and experience the positive effects of sexual energy on our bodies and our senses in ways that actually surpass the pleasure of orgasm.

Of course, there's nothing wrong with orgasm! Relaxing into sex does not mean denying our urges and never having an orgasm. Rather, it means sometimes *allowing* for the *even more profound and amazing feelings* you are capable of experiencing. It means harnessing your powerful life force, your sexual energy, and feeling better than you've ever imagined possible.

The next time you watch a movie or TV show where they cut to a scene moments after a couple has obviously just had sex, notice that, if they've supposedly had powerful, explosive sex and a wonderful time, they are huffing and puffing and maybe sweating and sighing. Or maybe they've had so-so sex and they are conflicted about finding themselves together. Hmmm … not much difference … still huffing, puffing, and sighing. The two have usually put some physical distance between them while they catch their breath and recoup their energies. They look exhausted. They may not even be looking at one another and have disconnected completely. They are like boxers who have gone back to their corners. And then … they go to sleep.

Sometimes the show has a scene leading up to sex that includes a desperate dance to the bedroom or couch, the partners lip-locked and shedding articles of clothing as they breathlessly make their way. Hurry. Hurry. Of course, this kind of quick, exciting, hot-and-bothered sex certainly has its place in anyone's sexual repertoire, but it is not the be-all and end-all of lovemaking. It is an example of turning sexual energy into excitement that is built up quickly, released quickly, and never harnessed to provide all the wonders that are available through true connection of spirit and body. As I said before, I bet you've always known there must be *more*. And you were right. There is so much more!

Spiritual lovemaking is more like a meandering walk in nature than a cruise down the information highway. Even if you have only a few minutes, using them to push to climax can ultimately leave you less relaxed than you will be if you use those minutes to really tune in and see what there is to experience in the short time you have with your lover. You may rise from a short encounter having engendered a good deal of sexual energy, and you and your partner may even still feel aroused, but at the same time you'll feel energized and, yes, relaxed, not depleted.

There is a difference between being excited and being energized. Sexual excitement can lead to a sudden crash and the empty feeling of "is that all?" Have you ever been extremely attracted to a partner, had "hot" sex, and finished, wondering what you'd been so fired up about in the first place? That's because you simply "fired off" your sexual excitement rather than truly mingling energies and forging a connection with your partner.

Once you reach a peak, there is no place to go but ... down! The peak of sexual excitement is always followed by a letdown. However, sexual *energy* can build endlessly without a fall.

Think of climbing a mountain trail with exquisite views. You power up to the first peak that you see in the near distance. When you get there, you say, "I've made it," and then you turn around and walk back down. This is analogous to conventional sex ending in orgasm. It may be wonderful and feel great. However ... now it's over. Once the peak has been reached, there is no place to go but back down.

Allowing Your Sexual Energy Free Rein

Spiritual sex shows you that you can walk steadily, mindfully, to that first peak, taking in the stream, trees, sky, and breeze, and when you get to that peak (which at first may have seemed like the ultimate "top"), you'll see off in the distance an even more gorgeous and inviting vista. You'll see new and higher peaks beckoning. Then, instead of turning back, off you'll go again, filled with even more awe and wonder, to the next peak, and the next ... never discharging and throwing away that amazing feeling, but rather letting it build. Never declaring yourself having "arrived," you'll allow the energy to build and continue to carry you along, even as it sometimes dips toward a valley, only to rise again toward an ever higher point. Valleys, twists, turns, more peaks.... no end! By relaxing into your walk, or into sex, and taking in every single tiny NOW moment, you'll open your eyes and your body to terrain that was invisible to you before.

If you live in a wooded or mountainous area, you know what I mean. You probably wouldn't go for the same twenty-minute walk each day. Instead, you'd explore the landscape. Up, down, around. Sometimes for hours on end. Sometimes lying down in a meadow and simply waiting for inspiration, and other times jogging merrily along a path. Spiritual sex allows the sexual energy free rein to give you the maximum experience your body and spirit are capable of. Once you've allowed yourself to follow the energy where it wants to take you, you'll not often settle for regular sexual excitement and orgasm anymore.

Peter:

When I remember what I used to think about the male sexual experience, I get an image of a roaring river. At the mouth of the river, the force of the water converges into a narrow outlet, which is dammed. Behind the dam, the pressure is constantly building and the water level is continually rising.

The dam bursts open.

Ejaculation brings such relief!

The pressure is released with a spectacular gushing of energy. Wow!

Then we enter into a sort of depleted splendor, and finally—usually—it's off to a very pleasant sleep.

That was good.

But here's something better.

Relaxed sex is a like an unrestricted river, continuously flowing, swirling, flushing, and rolling.

Letting go of your sexual oars and allowing yourself to simply float along this river of energy will leave you feeling invigorated and alive. Rather than ending your ride feeling done in, you will feel physically and spiritually refreshed.

Relaxed sex will put a spring in your step and a glow in your heart. And yet, when it's time for sleep, you'll find it easy to drift off into a deep, restorative slumber.

As your internal sexual-flow experience deepens, your desire for ejaculation will begin to dissipate. You will simply and naturally feel like going for it less and less often.

Make no mistake. There is no deprivation here. No going without. No pushing against of any kind. Rather, ejaculation simply won't be enough for you anymore! Sometimes, of course. But merely having an orgasm will quickly pale in comparison to the experience of being orgasmic.

The premise of *Spiritual Lovemaking* is so simple that it can be deceptive. It's just a basic change of mind from thinking of sex as an activity to thinking of lovemaking as the empowering of natural sexual energy. Sexual energy can and should be used to bring you closer to your partner than you ever imagined possible. It can be accessed to energize your entire life.

Sexual energy is a basic driving force in our human experience, yet few of us have made the effort to understand it, to use it, and to rejoice in it. Some of us have even tried to deny it. Relaxing and slowing down are the keys to tapping into the wonderful sexual life force energy and allowing it to work its magic.

CHAPTER THREE
Relaxation

When I asked several people what comes to mind when they hear the word *relax*, their answers did not surprise me. One said, "Sitting on my couch at home watching TV." Another said, "Riding my bike through the park." Another mentioned "cocktail hour." Still another said, "A long hot bubble bath." All of these are ways we might choose to get some recreation, get away from the daily grind, change direction, and let ourselves go a little. And yet how often when doing these things do we truly, deeply relax?

Check yourself next time you are lying on the sofa, playing a game, or socializing. You might be surprised to find that many parts of your body (and your mind) are tense and tight. And where is your mind while you are taking that bath? Are you really letting go of all thought and just relaxing? You may find that being truly quiet and deeply physically relaxed is something that eludes you. Perhaps that bath comes closest to the possibility of entering a calm, meditative state where our non-physical selves (thoughts and emotions) are in sync with our physical bodies, where we suspend time and just *be* rather than *do*.

Relaxation involves both the body and the mind. It entails letting go of thoughts, expectations, and goals, and letting the body achieve maximum comfort and ease.

Releasing Tension

Where there is tension there can be no relaxation. The two states of being are diametrically opposed. This seems obvious, and yet we often try to reach a relaxed state too quickly and do not honor the fact that the tension needs to be released in layers. It cannot be let go of all at once, even if we play a round of golf, drink a martini, or fire up the Jacuzzi. Relaxation isn't just the opposite of tension; it's a process, a journey. We need time and the mindset that we are worthy and enough even when we are not creating, not progressing, not *doing*.

So what does this have to do with sex?

We've all heard the term *sexual tension*. We intuitively and experientially understand that to have an orgasm we must build up tension and then release it. We experience sex as an excitement. We create this excitement by *doing*. This doing can take the form of creating stimulating thoughts with the mind or physically stimulating our bodies. We become more and more excited ... and more and more tense, as we build to a release. Often, however, after the momentary feel-good release, we experience depletion, even exhaustion, and rather than feeling refreshed and rejuvenated by sex, we feel tired and disappointingly empty.

Ejaculation is not relaxation. Ejaculation releases energy and dissipates it. The depletion that follows ejaculation is not the same as relaxation. A person can be in a state of full relaxation while holding the sexual energy within their body and not coming to orgasm. Relaxing into sex means harnessing the sexual energy and allowing it to energize and vitalize the body, rather than building it to an excited peak followed by a burst of release. This does not mean we want to bring ourselves to the verge of orgasm and hold it back, and it does not mean that we should try to maintain that fragile moment of excitement just before orgasm for long periods of time. These are misconceptions that sometimes surround the concept of Tantric sex.

During the highest-tension activity of the sex act, when we've created a lot of excitement due to action, we are disconnected from our partner and even from our inner self, while we focus on the area of tension and drive toward release. Once the point of no return is reached in our tense activity, orgasm is inevitable, and the sex act comes to its (sometimes involuntary) end. Often one partner reaches orgasm before the other, so that their ending is off balance, and sometimes one partner fails to reach the "goal" at all. As the sexual tension subsides, a feeling of release follows. This is not, however, a feeling of true relaxation.

Relaxing into sex offers a completely new (although surprisingly ancient) and different way of experiencing lovemaking.

Relaxed, spiritual lovemaking is making love without tense excitement.

Relaxed, spiritual lovemaking is making love with a focus on the present moment and the energy playing in our bodies and minds, and not on the release of that energy.

When we listen to the innate wisdom of our bodies, we are guided to allow our natural impulses to take over, and the act of sex becomes so much more than a simple creation of tension and release. We have the potential to experience infinitely more when we take the time to allow our bodies to do what they naturally know so well in the absence of goal-oriented action. It may take some practice to change this ingrained concept of thought, but if you think of it as a transformation from *doing* to *being*, you will be well on your way to experiencing sex in a far more satisfying and exciting way.

Be, don't *do*.

Being versus *doing* is a novel concept for some of us. It's hard to conceptualize that our bodies have inherent knowledge and that our minds do not have to control the experience of our bodies during lovemaking. We don't have to decide to "do this, and then do that …" in order to drive our bodies to a goal. This is perhaps a new departure: to accept that the body, when left to its own *being* devices, will *naturally* be drawn to the ecstatic heights of sexual feeling and will experience amazing physical pleasures that are available only when the mind is turned off and the spirit is tuned in.

Will you have orgasms when you relax? Yes, you will, whenever that is your choice. Your body knows what to do, and it will release sexual tension when necessary or when you simply decide that you want to experience an orgasm. However, the times when you allow orgasm not to be the goal, when you *relax* into sex and into *being* rather than *doing*, are the times that will transform your experience of sex and, potentially, even your entire life experience.

You may decide not to orgasm every time you make love. Your understanding of what your body is capable of feeling and your awareness of possibilities will expand exponentially. You will discover that you can achieve an *orgasmic state* even without the actual release and depletion of sexual energy of a physical orgasm. This orgasmic state arises from the sexual energy that moves through the body in waves when we experience sexual union from within the depths of pure relaxation and awareness.

The Power of True Relaxation

So, how can you harness this sexual energy by relaxing?

As you make love in conscious awareness, allow yourself to determine the exact moment when the desire for orgasm or ejaculation arises. Becoming aware of your proximity to the edge of the cliff is a significant step and allows you a choice as you make love. As you observe yourself becoming overwhelmed with excitement, you can step back a little and begin to play with your sexual energy. The usual choice at this point would be simply to follow the desire to fruition and continue to build up the excitement to the release of orgasm. If you do choose this, be aware that you are making the choice, and then remain conscious of that choice right to the end. This advice may seem to be aimed more at the man than the woman; however, the ability to reach this orgasmic state of connection is the same for both genders.

With focus, you can choose to retain the energy, taking it back in, inverting it, and recirculating it. We will discuss the process of relaxation in part 2 of this book, but for now, here is an overview of how you can harness the power of true relaxation.

Stop. Be still. Alone or with your partner, tune in to your own body for a moment. Relax the muscles of your spine, your belly, your buttocks, and even your feet. Feel your sexual energy as it infuses your being, leaving you energized and vital yet even more relaxed. Allow yourself to feel this fully. If you give this feeling your full attention and allow enough time, its intensity of pleasure might surprise you.

Most of us have always believed that a hard, erect penis is a minimum prerequisite for the pleasure of both partners in lovemaking. This is one of the most basic and unfortunate misunderstandings we can hold about sex. This may also be one of the most difficult concepts of relaxing into sex for you to accept—I know it was for me! And yet the simple truth is that the penis is a generative organ, no matter what state it is in. Hard or soft, it generates and exudes energy.

The body is designed to make love for hours and hours without ejaculation or orgasm. When a man ejaculates, sex is over for that session, and the opportunities for sharing and union have pretty much passed. So why not keep the energy moving and alive? Did you know that the penis can be inserted into the vagina without an erection? It can. And in fact this can prove to be one of the most satisfying experiences lovers can share. Allow yourself to be surprised. Keep your mind open and relaxed. I'll tell you more about this when we discuss soft penetration in part 2.

Setting the Stage for Lovemaking

Comfort is an important part of relaxation. Setting the stage for a session of spiritual lovemaking can make a world of difference. Especially when first trying out the idea of relaxed sex, making some initial preparations for the "duration" can be very helpful. Of course, the usual candles are nice, but you can do so much more to ensure the kind of comfort and ease that will allow you to truly relax into your experience and stay with it for a much longer amount of time than you are probably accustomed to allotting for lovemaking.

First, make sure children or pets are not in the vicinity and won't have to be looked after for a period of time. This may sound obvious, but as all parents know, true relaxation rarely occurs from the time of our child's birth until he or she leaves the nest unless we do some advanced planning. Yes, you can experience spiritual lovemaking while your child is asleep in the next room, but relaxed sex isn't a "quickie" that you engage in furtively.

Prepare a sacred space where you know you will not be interrupted. You do deserve this peaceful oasis. In fact, you will not be able to relax unless you prepare for lovemaking. Preparation is both physical and mental. Start hours before by going in your thoughts to the place where you will make love, and mentally pre-pave the experience with your positive expectations and anticipation. Imagine how relaxed you will feel. Imagine feeling joyful and alive and, yes, comfortable. Think about what you can do to increase the comfort of the bed or wherever it is that you usually make love with your partner. Bring extra cushions, and have a selection of blankets and sheets on hand. What will you be able to grab easily if you feel chilled? And will it be easy to uncover yourself if you feel warm?

Have a pitcher of water or other beverage on hand. Keep a natural lubricant, such as pure coconut oil, on both sides of the bed so that either partner can comfortably reach out for it. Coconut oil is ideal because it is taken in by the skin anywhere on the body and absorbed as a wonderfully nurturing and nourishing substance, while it affords a most pleasing but not "greasy" glide for massage, for penetration, or just for touch. It tastes wonderful, too!

Consider the lighting as well. Try not to make love in complete darkness or in glaring sunlight. Soft light is relaxing and yet will not make you sleepy. Experiment with candles or lamps until you achieve an ambience that invites you to relax.

You may feel silly making all these preparations to make love with a longtime partner, but now you are going to *relax* into sex, and preparing for comfort will signal your body and mind that something different is about to occur. You are settling in. You are getting ready to *be here now.*

Please turn off the television and your phone. Soft music can be either distracting or enhancing. Experiment to observe its effect on your relaxation.

When you undertake to really relax into sex, you will discover that each time you make love, the experience is a different and unique event. Even if you and your partner have grown weary of the same old sex act, when you embrace relaxation and presence, you will discover a renewed desire to unite sexually, time and time again, and for much longer periods. Relaxed sex can never grow old or repetitious. You will discover new and different ways of sexual expression that did not occur to you when you were action oriented, and you will be continually surprised at how your lovemaking unfolds in ever more creative and satisfying ways.

CHAPTER FOUR

Polarity

While men and women have differences of anatomy that we can't ignore, what may not be immediately obvious, and what many of us do not keep in mind, is that male and female are in fact polar opposites. The yin/yang, positive/negative, dynamic/receptive *opposite poles* of male and female are what make sexual union so magnetic, enjoyable, and natural.

Think of two magnets, opposite forces coming together with an irresistible and undeniable force of attraction.

Allowing Your Natural Polarity

When a man and a woman allow themselves to be authentically present, and when they tune in to the intuitive guidance of their physical bodies, they become exquisitely aware of their differences, their very polarity, and the natural flow of magnetic attraction between their opposite poles. This can open up a completely different understanding of the sexual act, and it will keep giving its gifts as more awareness is brought to this polarity as time goes on.

Note that homosexual couples also operate according to this concept of polarity. Like the ancient tantras, I refer to "the man" and "the woman" in this book, but it should be understood that the poles are always represented in every coupling if sex is satisfying. Polarity is a universal concept with regard to sexual activity and relationships. Ironically, gay couples may in fact find the concept of polarity less problematic. If they do not operate under the same worry about equality in the relationship, they are freer to be sexually polarized in ways that bring about stronger sexual attraction.

Most of us have come to believe that to emphasize the differences between the genders is to be politically incorrect. We have developed a fear that in affirming that we are different, we might inadvertently express that one gender is somehow superior to the other. In an effort to be correct and fair, we have done ourselves a disservice by negating the natural and satisfying ways in which men and women *are* different and distinct male and female entities.

Sex and lovemaking are not the same as driving a car or conducting a board meeting. We have no need to make a conscious decision to negate the innate differences between the genders; in fact, when we do so, we limit our ability to reach the heights of pleasure our bodies can provide. An important part of relaxing into sex is relaxing into our male or female identity, naturally accepting the differences between us and reveling in those differences.

Male and female are indeed equal, but they are not the same. Think of the ancient Chinese symbol for yin and yang. The two sides are distinct, different, and opposite, yet they fit together elegantly to form a perfect whole. Male energy coincides with the Eastern concept *yang*, while female energy coincides with *yin*. These polar opposites attract each other in sublime and amazing ways when not thwarted by thought or action. When we allow our natural polarity, we are in balance.

Balance feels relaxing.

And we relax into balance.

Igniting Natural Magnetic Attraction Through Polarity

The dance of being what we really are happens without effort, without force. In fact, by forcing ourselves to perform almost identical sexual behaviors and believing we must be the same to be equal, we disconnect from our authentic beings, preventing the fullness of what is possible for us to enjoy in lovemaking.

By remaining fully conscious and aware of our bodies while allowing them their natural polarity, we set in motion the powerful electromagnetic forces that bring about sexual union. By deliberately and calmly focusing inward, we bring polarity to our awareness, and this evokes a feeling of powerful attraction to our opposite, our partner. When the female partner fully allows her authentic feminine self to be present and the male allows the totality of his masculinity to come forth, the lovers are drawn ever more powerfully into sexual union.

So we see that being polar opposites makes us more compatible, not less! Male sexual energy is essentially the positive pole, while female energy represents the negative pole. Each must be activated in order to bring about the natural magnetic attraction. It also bears noting that, while men are positively charged, they also carry within them an inner negative pole, and women likewise carry an inner positive pole. This means that in the absence of a partner, we are not incomplete beings, and we can each generate a complete circuit of sexual energy. However, with a partner, when we allow our natural polarity to lead, we can achieve a most ecstatic and intense union.

The male body carries the positive pole in the genital area, while the female positive pole is in the breasts and heart area. The male negative pole resides in his chest and heart, while the female negative pole is in her genitals. A natural and very powerful magnetic field exists between the positive and negative poles. When bodies meet, coming together at opposite poles, the "electrical circuit" closes and completes itself. Male energy is introduced from the penis into the vagina and flows upward toward the woman's heart. Female sexual energy flows from the breasts and heart into the heart area of the man and down to his penis. This circle of energy is a powerful spiritual as well as physical force.

Nurturing Polarity During Lovemaking

Respecting and understanding this energetic polarity has a profound effect on lovemaking. When man and woman come together, their positive poles are usually already awake and ready. Typically, when a man achieves an erection, he is ready to have it touched and attended to, and most of us have learned to assume that its counterpart, the clitoris or vaginal area, can or should be similarly activated simultaneously. When we understand polarity, however, we realize that the positive pole in the woman is her breasts, not her genitals. When the breasts are given attention, warmed, and loved, they start the energy moving along the circuit, and soon enough the vagina, the woman's negative pole, comes to life with electric charge, inviting the penis to unite with it.

When we understand polarity, we realize that what men have learned about immediately stimulating the clitoris can often be too much too soon. The clitoris and vagina belong to the woman's negative pole, and they will awaken naturally when the energy travels down to them from the positive pole, the breasts and heart area, which should be awakened first. This simple concept alone can be refreshingly helpful to couples that have been frustrated by our modern misunderstandings of the differences in response between the genders. Understanding polarity puts everything in a new light.

As a man and a woman come together for lovemaking, as they relax and give loving attention to one another's positive poles first, they will see that the body's intelligence and natural electromagnetic nature will take over, starting the travels of sexual energy toward the negative poles so that when they naturally and irresistibly come together, polarity will already be fully activated.

In sexual union, the feminine partner is the natural receiver and the masculine is the natural giver. Male strength and clarity of purpose are appropriate in lovemaking to maintain polarity.

The woman can relax into her natural desire to be softer and more feminine, bringing her into balance against the man's energies. Please understand that we are not saying that softness and receptivity are the same as subordination and passivity! Polarity does not demand that the woman be physically passive during lovemaking or that the man must always "make the moves," and it should be clear that the sexual dance sometimes changes leaders during lovemaking. However, the basic concept of polarity, which is an energetic flow of positive and negative, should always be taken into account.

Through allowing this intrinsic polarity, we relax more deeply.

We can relax when we realize that all we need to do is be ourselves and follow our natural inclinations. The more polarity is allowed, the more powerful the sexual sensations will be. The potential of polarity is truly limitless when we do not push against it in thought or action.

Once the circuit is closed and the opposite poles have come together, if the partners remain relaxed and continue to allow the energy to circulate freely, even higher frequencies of electric charge between the poles will occur.

Without allowing polarity, attraction cannot occur, and coming together will feel forced and unsatisfying. Illustrate this to yourself by thinking again of two magnets. It is impossible to force the magnets to unite at their identical poles, yet they literally cannot help but unite, naturally, at their opposite poles. So it is with lovemaking. Nurture polarity. Allow it. Go with its flow, and your bodies will show you what is naturally possible when nothing is forced. Take the time to warm up the positive poles and then the negative in each partner, and always ... relax.

Think about your partnership with your lover. If the woman uses masculine energy in her job and in her day-to-day tasks, and if the man uses his feminine side more and more often, then relaxing into your natural sexual polarity for lovemaking can be a delicious relief.

Some relationships change over time, and the partners often find the reasons mysterious. Consider that when lovers first meet and become attracted to one another, the woman is in her feminine energy, and the man is in his masculine energy. As time goes by, a subtle, unconscious shift can take place to the point where polarity is neutralized. Once polarity is neutral, a deep love and appreciation may still exist, but sexual intimacy will cease. When lovemaking is put by the wayside, the connection between the partners loosens, and resentments and misunderstandings may abound. If you suspect this shift has happened in your relationship, try to consciously allow polarity to come back. For more information on how to do this in your relationship outside of lovemaking, refer to material by David Deida mentioned in the resource section at the end of this book.

In lovemaking, polarity must be maintained for attraction. Relaxing and just being, without doing, is a giant step toward restoring polarity. Think of those magnets again. One partner must maintain more masculine energy, and the other more feminine. Relax. Be yourself.

CHAPTER FIVE

Awareness

Perhaps you're acquainted with the messages and books of some of the spiritual teachers of today. They speak of being here now and remaining present in your experience. Many of us jokingly refer to the fact that we have only the *now*, yet how many of us really understand and implement this concept in our lives? You may have undertaken to be here now, focusing on the present moment, but with varying success. After all, in some aspects of life, goals are necessary, and driving, future-oriented action taken toward realizing them is encouraged and appropriate.

Be Here Now

The lesson, however, is in learning to *be here now*, whether or not you are involved in physical action. It is in being open to the voice of your inner guidance and to the nuances of your experience. This doesn't mean you must lie down and be motionless and still; rather, it means you can stop your thinking and planning enough to feel, experience, and be, in the moment. You can do this even while you are moving and doing. Your movements and actions will be more like a fluid dance than a robotic body taking orders from the mind. You can say, "I'm sweeping the garage right now. This is how my arm muscle feels as I press the broom onto the floor. This is how the birds sound, and I hear the sound of some children playing in the distance. The air is still and sweet, and I am taking a deep breath as I move around the garage. I am calmly noticing my surroundings, and as I relax into this task, I am inspired to take actions that didn't occur to me this morning when I planned this chore."

You do have a goal: seeing the garage organized and immaculate at the end of the day. But what *be here now* asks is that you make the main experience the series of present moments, and not the future goal. You can end up standing exhausted and depleted in the tidy garage, or you can stand exhilarated, calm, and energized when your project is completed. It's all in how you have experienced the task, the moment-by-moment *being* in the task. If you make it your intention to be aware and conscious as you undertake something, you will experience it entirely differently than if you focus your intention solely on the end result, or even on what comes next, and next, and next.

I don't mean that cleaning the garage is necessarily analogous to having sex with your partner. I want to drive home the point that no matter what you are *doing*, it's how you are *being* that defines your experience. How you feel in any given moment is far less dependent on circumstances or your actions than on your awareness, your consciousness, and your presence.

The joy is in the journey, not the destination.

Is this true?

I'm sure you've heard this popular wisdom many times, in many ways. It's only partially true, however, and in spiritual lovemaking, we realize that for the best experience, there is no need even for a journey! A journey implies movement from point A to point B. It has a beginning and an end and usually has a destination. In relaxed, spiritual sex, there is no goal. There is no "going somewhere." There is only the immediate moment. The now.

During spiritual lovemaking, we are not on a "journey to orgasm." The message of relaxing into sex is not "enjoy each moment on the way to climax." Rather, it is "enjoy each moment." We may, as we experience a series of "nows," reach orgasm, just as while we meander down a path in the woods, the path may end at a friend's cottage or a waterfall. Spiritual lovemaking is asking you to go nowhere, and simply experience the moment to its fullest, rather than think about going toward any end at all. You will still "journey," but not purposefully. While making love, you can remain present in every single moment, not looking toward an ending but just being and experiencing all of the nuances and listening to your body's natural guidance. Then, whether you end up having an orgasm or not, you'll emerge from the lovemaking session with a renewed and energized body and mind.

Just this morning before settling in to write, as I habitually do, I took a walk in the woods just outside the front door. I love the changing seasons and how different the walk seems each day, even though I often walk the same paths each morning. This morning I noticed I was almost home again, after forty-five minutes of walking, and had not experienced the walk. I realized all at once that during most of my hike I was not "here now," but rather somewhere else (at my laptop?) in my mind, and I had *missed* almost the entire experience! If there had been lovely clouds, chirping birds, even a rabbit along the way—if the crisp fall leaves had crunched under my shoes, and if there had been a soft breeze blowing the few leaves left on the trees down into my path—I had not seen those things. Perhaps I had seen them with my eyes, but I had not experienced them because my mind was future oriented, thinking about this chapter and beyond.

There could be no better validation for me of how easy it is to slip into thinking about future goals and miss the present. The present is really all we actually have to experience, so don't miss it! Don't miss the smallest sensations and the most powerful energies that pass between you and your lover *now* because you are focused on getting somewhere or getting something right.

Spiritual lovemaking is about being here now. It is a relaxation of the mind and an opening of the spirit. It is allowing the body's own intelligent guidance to take over. This guidance will come from your conscious awareness, which as you relax you will come to know as distinct from your thinking mind. By slowing down and simply being, your conscious awareness can be deliberately awakened, and it will guide you easily and naturally. The art of spiritual lovemaking affords an intense sexual experience and asks for the complete relaxation of body and mind. It is a transcending of the mundane, yet is absolutely accessible to each of us.

Relaxed sex brings lovemaking into the realm of meditation. As we discussed in chapter 1, the physical experience is actually part of the spiritual experience. It is the combination of both physical and spiritual that makes us whole.

Being consciously aware of the present moment means letting go of the creation of thought. Being *aware* means keeping ourselves open to our ever-present and constant inner wisdom. You may never have tried meditation, or you may meditate regularly but have never really related it to sex. If you are new to the idea of letting go and stopping thought, try to relax into this new idea and give it a chance.

You really do have control over your mind, and as you gently intend to stop your mind from creating thought while you are making love, your intention will be successful in time. If you are adept at meditation, you'll readily see how your lovemaking will improve as you apply the principle *be here now* to sex with your partner. Everything takes on a certain glow and clarity as you remain more and more present and accounted for in your life. As you make love, when you are relaxed and in the moment, not moving relentlessly toward a goal, you become engulfed in the magic. The world sparkles, and you feel fresh and whole.

The awareness that relaxing into sex asks of you is an opening to consciousness. It is an allowing of your whole being to simply *be*... rather than *do*. Consciously making love means that you are exquisitely aware of every nuance, every slight movement, every sound, taste, and touch. This awareness makes the difference between a purely sexual act and an act of love and joy.

In meditation, awareness is turned inward. We stop thought and become conscious only of our inner life, our *being*. You need not be completely still to be in a meditative state. When you move your body in a relaxed and conscious manner and you allow your awareness to be acute yet grounded in the here and now, you will be making love in meditation. As long as your consciousness remains quiet and serene, your body can be moving, touching, sensing, and enjoying.

Awareness of Self During Lovemaking

The first step in total awareness is awareness of self.

We have been led to believe by the traditional (modern) thought on sex that to be a good lover, we need to focus on what our partner is feeling. We're taught not to be selfish in sex. We're taught to do things to excite our partner. In part this may be the reason sex becomes a chore for so many couples, not because they do not desire to please one another—they do—but rather because they feel insecure in their ability to do it time and time again. We wonder if letting go of the actions we have learned to take to stimulate our partner will make us seem selfish or disinterested. When we see sex as a behavior, a set of actions, we are trapped in the "I have to do it right every time" box, and begin to find excuses not to have sex at all. Once we understand, however, that to be truly present for a lover means being present for the self first and foremost, we are free to relax into it.

Before asking yourself how your partner feels—whether what you are doing is good for your partner or whether you are doing things right—try asking, "What do *I* feel?" Set an intention to bring your full awareness to each of your own body parts. Be aware of each sensation, and ask yourself how you feel. By paying attention to yourself, you actually activate your body in ways that will satisfy your partner by association.

Making love to a partner who is disconnected from his or her own sensations feels wooden and inauthentic. Don't use frantic action to cover up disconnection. Don't be afraid to relax into consciousness and remain selfishly aware of your own experience. Focus on the joy that being near your partner's body provides. Focus on how it makes *you* feel to touch and be touched. Focus on how it makes *you* feel to take in your lover's scent, feel the smoothness of your lover's skin, and hear the sounds of your lover's breathing or sighs. This powerful step in awareness can change everything.

To facilitate this awareness, we must relax. For some of us, the art of physical relaxation is one we lost somewhere early in childhood. We might not even be familiar with the way our body feels when we fully allow ourselves to let go and relax. Awareness and relaxation go hand in hand. As you set the intention to be aware and conscious, you will naturally relax, and as you relax, your awareness will be heightened. Keep practicing and intending, and each time you make love, you'll find yourself giving way to deeper relaxation and awareness.

Remember, let go of your mind and allow your body to do all the "thinking." Feel. Be. Relax. Pull your attention inward to ever more minute details and shades of feeling. Pull your attention from the general toward the specific. Notice details you were too preoccupied to notice before.

Aware. "What am I feeling?"

Relaxed. Let go of any tension, one muscle at a time.

Conscious. Pay attention to your own sensations. Don't think. Just be and feel.

Relaxed. Let go of tension. Face, shoulders, back...

Aware. "What am I feeling?"

When you feel you've achieved a level of relaxation and awareness that is a bit deeper than you've experienced previously, allow yourself to rest there, enjoying it, feeling it in every cell of your body. Be present in it.

Now notice how, as you hold your focus on this feeling of relaxation, it naturally expands.

Your heartbeat, the sounds in your environment, the sounds your bodies make, your breathing... notice these, and become exquisitely aware of each in turn as you continue to focus on your own sensory experience.

By giving time and attention to the way your own body feels, you become a much more welcoming and open partner. Your lover will sense your strong, aware, and conscious being and will be drawn powerfully into its magnetic field.

Slow down your movements. Don't worry that you'll end up doing "nothing." You will move. And when you do, your movements will be in response to your deep awareness of what your body is experiencing. Your movements will be slow, graceful, and fluid—not goal oriented or purposeful. You won't have to use thought to direct your movements. They will arise naturally, ecstatically.

Don't be worried if you simply lie still for longer periods of time than would previously have been comfortable for you. This doesn't mean you are losing interest or have become an inactive or ineffectual partner. Allow yourself to be still yet open to impulses to move. They will come naturally as you remain in conscious awareness of the present moment. Remember, lovemaking has no goal. Being aware of the power of sexual union and being awake to its every sensation, you will find yourself in an uninhibited state of joyful intimacy with your partner.

An Exercise in Awareness for Spiritual Lovemaking

This exercise was adapted from *The Heart of Tantric Sex* by Diana Richardson. As Diana says, we have become *human doings* and forgotten how to be *human beings*. Try this exercise with your partner to help you reconnect with your ability to just be.

As a prelude to making love, lie on your sides and face each other, keeping your bodies inches apart, with no physical contact. Close your eyes, and focus on your own body. Pull your awareness toward what you are feeling. Imagine your own sexual energy traveling through your body, from the top of your back down to the base of your body and your legs. Give yourself time to hold your awareness there for several moments before you bring your bodies together.

Then open your eyes and look at each other, all the while keeping your awareness on your own sensations. Relax your jaw. Breathe. Allow a few moments to pass in this relaxation before slowly, very slowly, inching toward each other and meeting in a slow embrace. Start with just a meeting of the fingertips, and naturally and slowly let your bodies come together. Rather than "doing" this embrace, try to allow it to "happen." Stay aware of each of your body parts and what each one is feeling. You and your partner will be naturally and easily attracted to each other, like magnets. Allow yourself to just "be" as this occurs of its own accord. Moving into lovemaking with this slow, languid sensitivity allows a vibrant, expansive experience.

The Role of Sexual Fantasy

Being aware and conscious requires turning off our thinking mind. In the heightened state of conscious awareness during relaxed sex, we are not doing and creating but rather are noticing and being. This means that we are not even creating thoughts!

So the question might arise: What about fantasy?

Conventional thought holds that sexual fantasy is desirable. We are encouraged to conjure fantasies even when we are enjoying sex with a partner. The idea is that anything goes in an effort to become as sexually excited as possible. After all, when the goal of sex is to reach a peak of tension and to orgasm as strongly as possible, exciting and arousing thoughts can be tools to get us there.

Relaxed sex is different. You are not trying to achieve a goal. Only the joy and satisfaction of the present exist, so escaping to another place or time is unnecessary, since the actual experience you are having is so exquisite when you take it in through your newly relaxed attitude.

Fantasy is the *deliberate creation of thoughts*, and it removes us from our awareness of the here and now. This approach cuts us off from much of what is spiritual and powerful about lovemaking. When we are thinking thoughts—especially thoughts that take us away from the current moment, away from what is happening *now*—we remove ourselves from present awareness and consciousness, and we literally "leave the building."

Relaxed sex does not require fantasy, because it is grounded right here and has no goal. During spritual love-making, we intensely feel what is happening in the present moment. We are open to experiencing the moment to absolute fullness and to achieving the most rejuvenating and ecstatic union possible.

Activate Your Imagination

Imagination, like fantasy, entails focusing our thoughts. Imagination and fantasy are not the same, however. When we fantasize, we use the mind to take us somewhere else. By calling forth the power of imagination, however, we can enhance the here and now.

Sexual union is a perfect time to activate your imagination.

Relax.

Switch off creative thoughts and allow your authenticity to surface. Direct your imagination inward and, remaining in the here and now, picture the flow of sexual energy through your body. Imagine energy flowing between you and your partner. Envision your sexual feelings as a golden glow or light, and consciously flow it through your body and outward toward your lover. Imagine that the feelings you are having right now are becoming more and more powerful, expanding and amplifying into ecstasy. Picture energy leaping from the penis and flowing up to the breasts. Use your imagination, but don't go on a trip in your mind. Be here. Now. Don't think about where you are going. There is no destination. You have already arrived and are present in a delicious and satisfying moment.

Remember, lovemaking is not a performance. It is not a sport. You have nothing to prove and no end to achieve. You will always "succeed," because the purpose is pure enjoyment and the expression of love. You don't need to do a thing. Just relax. Feel. Be.

CHAPTER SIX

The Universal Law of Attraction

Your partner can love you only as much as you love yourself.

Like many profound truths that are potentially life changing, this is actually a difficult concept for most of us to grasp. You might be reading this and saying, "Love myself? Well, sure I do, but I don't want to be *selfish*." In fact, we've had the evils of "selfishness" drilled into us so firmly that feelings of almost any kind of entitlement—even the basics of love, acceptance, and joy—have been drilled *out!* We've been taught to look for validation and acceptance from others before we will give them to ourselves.

Most of us have been taught that we have to perform according to a certain standard in order to make the grade, and that it's always someone else making the call as to whether we're measuring up. That "someone else" changes according to the situation and where we are in life, but there always seems to be someone else we have to please before we can truly accept and love ourselves.

It's not surprising that in our primary romantic, sexual, and life-partner relationships, we often trust the judgment of our partner before we check in with our own feelings and innate knowledge of our self-worth. At times, even if we are aware that our partner's feelings and opinions are at odds with our own, we'll still speak and behave in accordance with theirs, to keep the peace or to make them happy. We may do this with family members or even mere acquaintances. Sometimes, even unawares, we keep repeating this behavior over and over again in hopes that it will yield the results we want so much. We keep hoping that in return for all this pleasing, we'll win the prize of true acceptance from others. Never really thinking about it much, we assume self-acceptance will follow.

The reason this never works is because of the law of attraction.

Like Attracts Like

The law of attraction states that whatever comes into our experience is in response to our own alignment. In other words, we will experience only that with which we are energetically aligned.

Some state the law this way: "Like attracts like." I can see you rolling your eyes and asking, "Well, why did I just learn about polarity, where opposites attract, only to be told that it's really all about attraction between two things that are alike?" There is no contradiction here, because the spiritual precept that "like attracts like" applies to energy resonance, or vibration. I know it's tricky, but the negative and positive poles of the magnets we talked about in chapter 4 are actually vibrating synchronistically at the same frequency, so they attract each other.

Energy vibrates. Matter vibrates. You vibrate—and I mean both your physical and non-physical aspects are vibrating—all the time. Those vibrations are bringing to you vibrationally resonant people, things, and experiences. You are attracting to you the people, things, and experiences that vibrationally match the way *your* energy is vibrating with regard to all people, things, and experiences.

The law of attraction is universal, and there are no exceptions. We attract into our lives something energetically similar to whatever our non-physical selves are aligned with. Remember, we said that our spiritual selves are made up of our non-physical aspects—that is, our thoughts, feelings, and emotions. These non-physical aspects, for the purpose of our discussion, make up our spirit, or soul, and whatever we've aligned them with is what we'll attract more of into our physical experience.

Let's try to illustrate this concept further and bring it back to lovemaking. Let's say my physical self is all ready to make love. I've taken a bath, lit a candle, and readied the coconut oil, and I'm waiting for my lover. And let's say that as I go about this preparation, I'm envisioning myself being gazed on and accepted with appreciation and love. I'm picturing it in my mind and feeling it with my emotions, which is the same as saying that I'm aligning my non-physical self (my thoughts, feelings, and emotions) with this vision. I believe it is about to happen just as I want it to. I am open to an experience as good or even better than I can imagine. I am already living it in my creative mind, so the law of attraction will match me up with an experience that is *in resonance* with my thoughts and emotions.

On the other hand, I could have performed all of the exact same physical preparations and been physically more ready than ever to receive my partner and engage in amazing lovemaking, BUT what if all the while, instead of thinking about how wonderful it was going to be, I'd been worrying, "Will he think I'm fat?" What if I'd been thinking that I wasn't lovable or attractive enough? What if I aligned my non-physical creative powers with the thought, "I don't think I'm a good enough lover"? What would be vibrating in resonance with those thoughts? Well, regardless of the good intentions of my partner, who cannot create in my experience, I would attract an encounter that was a match for those negative, non-self-accepting thoughts. This means he would be literally unable to show me any action, word, or emotion that did not match.

We keep looking for evidence of our being "okay" in our partner's eyes, or touch, or words, when in truth our lover can only be a reflection of what we are radiating out, of what we are a vibrational match with.

Truly, because the highest spiritual law—the law of attraction—is always at work, my lover can love me only as much as I love myself. Or, more accurately, I can experience love from my partner, or from anyone else, only in the exact measure that I experience my own love for myself. Anything else others may be offering will fall by the wayside; it will not be in resonance with me, and therefore I will not know or feel it.

Think about how powerful knowing this can make us. The power to create our own reality is almost too good to be true. Yet it's the way things work, and we have only to harness this power in order to bring everything we desire into our experience, not the least of which is amazing spiritual lovemaking.

The law of attraction can be hard to accept at first when we try to fit it into the paradigm I just outlined, where we are judged and found worthy or unworthy by those outside of ourselves. But think of it this way: If we've aligned with "I'm not good enough," then that's what we'll receive— more people, things, and experiences that will "validate" that alignment, that will "match" it. If we've aligned with an appreciation for our bodies and what they are capable of in lovemaking—the giving and receiving of love, affection, sexual joy, and satisfaction—then that is what we'll see reflected in our lover's eyes, body, and experience.

Notice how often your own estimation of intrinsic goodness goes up or down in response to what another is thinking and feeling (or in response to what you believe the person is thinking and feeling). Sometimes the discrepancy between what we feel about ourselves when we're being regarded with love, and what we feel when we are being ignored or regarded with harshness, can be so large as to be the difference between self-love and self-loathing. Yet, the truth is, the love we are receiving, the acceptance and the positive regard that flows to us, does so in response to what we are putting out into the world energetically. So we can become trapped in a vicious cycle of exchange of judgment. You can break this cycle by trying something new: Focus on self-love, and watch the results unfold.

Your Thoughts Have Creative Power

The law of attraction is sometimes stated this way:

You get what you think about.

I know, if you are reading this for the first time, you are raising an eyebrow at that one. After all, you might say, you think about money all day and yet you never seem to have any. Or perhaps you say, "I think about sex constantly, but my partner is hardly ever interested." Yet the statement "You get what you think about" is true!

Let's take the case of money first. The person who says he thinks all day every day about money, yet doesn't have any, is likely indeed having many thoughts about money— but they are negative and fearful thoughts about finances, and not positive, exciting, and liberating thoughts of abundance. Yes, "money" may be practically all he thinks about, but we create our reality through the vibration of our thoughts, not our words. Thoughts have power and non-physical energy attached to them. Thoughts vibrate. They are creative. And if those money thoughts are vibrating in sync with fear and lack, then more fear and lack are what will be attracted. Remember, "like attracts like" applies to the resonance of energy, not to the particulars of our thoughts.

Moving back to sex, if I am *hoping* that the sex will be good, or if I'm worrying about whether my lover can or will provide what I need, then those thoughts vibrate with the resonance of "I don't have what I need" and "I can't be sure things will be good for me." In this case, the law of attraction will deliver more "I don't have it" and more "I can't be sure." It's subtle, but when you grasp this concept and begin to align your thoughts, feelings, and emotions with what you *do* desire, and you devote more than 51 percent of your thoughts to aligning with your true desires and your real knowledge of your own power, then your life cannot help but open up and shift in amazing and wonderful ways.

So keep this truth in mind: "My lover can love me only as much as I love myself." When you come to your spiritual lovemaking session with thoughts of love for yourself, when you truly believe that you are worthy of love, and when you accept complete responsibility for your pleasure, then your energy will vibrate in resonance with your lover's matching response.

Let's keep the cycle of love going. Spiritual lovemaking will make this happen for you. Make this your mantra: "My lover can love me only as much as I love myself."

Breaking the Cycle of Judgment and Non-Acceptance

I know you may be thinking that it's just not that simple. You might say that you cannot simply decide in the moment to love yourself completely and have that love take hold in an instant. And I would agree that you will not traverse the distance from a deep feeling of inadequacy to a total knowledge of your precious and worthy place in the universe in just a moment.

The good news is that you do not have to go any distance to break the cycle of judgment and non-acceptance and to experience the joys of give and take of mutual unconditional love. All you have to do to make this a reality is to heed what spiritual lovemaking is asking you to do— that is, release any expectation that sex is an "activity," and simply relax into sex as a "state of mind."

Use the nine keys to spiritual lovemaking in part 2 of this book to help you focus into the here and now. When you are suspended in the here and now during lovemaking, with no place to go, no goal, and nothing to prove, you are free. When there is nothing you have to do, nothing you have to show for yourself, nothing you have to do, or be, or give, or live up to, you are free. You don't have to have an orgasm, and you don't have to provide one for your partner. You don't have to feel anything in particular.

When you float in this space of non-judgment and non-effort, inevitably you will start to emit the energetic message "I am love, I love you, and I love myself." You will *resonate* with the vibration of self-love. Why? Because this is your *nature*. It is the truth that your innermost being knows, and when all of the noise of what you've learned to the contrary is allowed to fade away, you will easily fall back into your natural ability to vibrate in sync with love, acceptance, and non-judgment. Almost as if by magic, you will become a magnet for the same acceptance and love that you are putting out. When you are in a state of mind where there is nothing whatever to prove to yourself or to your lover, there will suddenly be nothing for your lover to prove to you. Neither of you needs to do, be, or say anything in order to bathe in the light of acceptance and grace.

The amazing part is, this happens without effort, without planning, without design. You simply let go and allow yourself to *be* rather than do. This simple letting go aligns you with all that is love, so the "real" you can rise to the surface.

I know that while what I'm telling you here is simple, it may not be easy to do at first. It may take some practice and perseverance. However, to tempt you to try it, let me explain that when you practice letting go for even the smallest of time periods—perhaps just a second or two— your energy will begin to align with the vibration of love. Then each time you try it again, it will become more and more of a habit, and your being will come to recognize and gravitate toward the letting go more easily and quickly. Don't give up. You can align. Alignment of this kind means your physical and non-physical aspects have become one, and when this happens, you have only the ability to attract love and all else that you desire.

To bring home this point even more clearly, I'm going to give you some statements to think about. The following exercise is powerful and may reveal far more than you might guess. So give it a chance, and commit to making a change in your spirit (your thoughts, feelings, and beliefs) that will allow the law of attraction to bring you more of what you want.

An Exercise in Leveraging the Power of the Law of Attraction

Fill in the blanks in the way that is most meaningful and true for you right now. Be honest, and make the statements sound like the thoughts you usually think.

1. I don't like when my partner _____.

2. I'm afraid my partner _____.

3. I'm afraid that I _____.

4. When my partner doesn't _____, I don't feel loved.

5. When my lover says _____, I don't feel seen and accepted.

6. I need my partner to _____ in order to feel sexually turned on.

7. I want my lover to _____.

8. My partner never _____.

9. My partner always _____.

10. I wish my partner would _____.

Now, rewrite each statement in a way that aligns your spirit to leverage the power of the law of attraction. You don't have to do this all at once. Try one per day. Take your time, and give it some thought.

For example, for number 4, I wrote:

"When my partner doesn't show me a lot of physical affection, I don't feel loved."

To make this work for me, and to put out a vibration that matches what I want to attract, I might change this to:

"I am loved. I love giving and receiving physical affection. I adore the feelings of acceptance and love that receiving affectionate gestures gives me. I am a match for affection of all kinds."

Keep your new thoughts in the present tense. Start writing the new thoughts quickly, letting them flow. You can edit and rewrite until you have thoughts that really feel good. Don't worry if the new thoughts don't ring true just yet. You're going to "fake it till you make it" just a little bit. When you think these thoughts, remain present in the now, and try to feel the emotion of what you are asking for.

It's important that you stay with the new thought just as long as it feels good to think it. When you feel yourself drifting back to doubt, or putting in the "what ifs" or "buts," stop the exercise and come back to it later.

Be sure to make the distinction between thoughts that describe what you *do want* and thoughts that describe what you *don't want*. For example, look at the two thoughts I often found myself thinking: "I love physical affection, but my lover just doesn't do that" and "I wish he'd just give me a hug once in a while without my asking." These are actually thoughts that describe the *lack* of what I wanted. And thinking them, by the power of the law of attraction, actually brought me *more lack*!

Remember, then, that when you align your thoughts and emotions with what feels good, you are doing it for the good feeling that ensues. You don't have to think, "I'm creating what I want. I'm creating what I want." When you already have what you want in your thoughts and emotions, you have achieved it. The physical manifestation will follow, but what you really want, the feeling of it, has already been achieved.

Keep working at this exercise. You can do it without writing, too. Focus on what you do want, on what feels good, and practice transforming your observation of anything unwanted into a vision of what is wanted. It WILL become second nature to flip your thoughts to those that create what you want in sex, in love, and in life.

If exercises seem too much like homework to you, and you'd rather just keep reading, that's fine as well. Often in this book I'll tell you to be "goal-less." Yes, usually this refers to the "goal" of conventional sex: orgasm. However, there is danger in setting a new, more spritual-sounding goal to replace it. Try not to make "achieving alignment with your non-physical self" a kind of goal that entails success or failure. If you must have a purpose, make it "be here now," and alignment will follow. I promise.

CHAPTER SEVEN

Making the Change to Relaxed Sex

Making love in a relaxed, conscious, spiritual way is probably new for you. It may even be a complete and radical departure from everything you previously thought of as good sex. Change can be exciting, but it's not always easy and immediate, so it's fine to take small steps toward the relaxed way. Each time you do bring more conscious awareness and relaxation to sex, you will have taken another step on the journey to changing your life—all aspects of your life—for the better.

It may seem obvious to say that you bring your awareness everywhere you go, and perhaps even more obvious to say that you bring your body everywhere you go. However, when you learn to bring *awareness of your body* into every aspect of your daily experience, you'll have stepped into a realm few achieve. You'll find that no matter what your day-to-day endeavors may be, they will blossom and expand and feel more real. Whatever you attempt will be easier and more flowing, and your goals will be achieved with less effort and angst. The simple practice of *being here now* will change not only the way you make love but also every other activity of your body and mind.

We modern humans have become wary of stillness. To do nothing at all seems worse than doing something wrong! We've been taught to be creative, industrious, and success oriented in all we do—and we've included sex and love-making in that lot. Relaxation, we learn, must be earned. We have come to think of relaxing as what one does after work, not before or during. Similarly, we think of relaxation as coming *after* orgasm, not before or during. We've sadly limited ourselves and our potential for connection and joy by heeding these (new and modern) rules. When you relax into sex, you give your body an opportunity to feel all it was capable of feeling yet missed when you were on that willful course to orgasm—or worse, when you gave up on love-making as a major part of your connection to your partner.

What we are offering here is nothing short of revolutionary, although this knowledge is thousands of years old. It's fine to start slowly. You may want to begin by explor-ing one of the keys to spiritual lovemaking in part 2 of this book. Practice. If you often find your body striving toward orgasm, as it's been accustomed to doing, that's fine too. Allow and enjoy. Each step in changing will bring benefits, and they will accumulate and build on one another.

As you learn to retain and recirculate your powerful sexual energy, you'll find that making love will leave you energized for days afterward. You'll make love for hours and hours on end, and the glow of satisfaction and love will stay with you.

The relaxed, easy contentment you'll feel will infuse your life with a vitality you may never have known before.

When beginning to make the change to relaxed sex, it's natural to feel a little silly or even embarrassed. We are not used to quiet, do-nothing moments where all that is required is that we feel and tune in to our own sensations. You might experience outbreaks of laughter or even tears. Allow these! Tears and laughter are natural releasers of tension, and as you cry and laugh together, valleys of deeper relaxation will open to you.

What about passion?

Remember the TV and movie scenes mentioned in chapter 2? Would you say the characters are passionate? Not necessarily. They are excited, of course, but actually it's common to mistake urgent sexual desire for passion. True passion arises from a deep, sincere exuberance. True passion is strong feeling that is fully sustained for a period of time. Passion is deeply felt emotion. It is not measured by the presence of noisy flurries of activity. It will not burn out in an instant, but rather it will grow and become stronger as you allow yourself to access your depths. Passion can be felt in a positive or negative way. Even anger can be passionate. Passion will arise as you relax into sex. It doesn't have to entail sweating and panting, and it certainly doesn't mean you have to hurry!

Be authentic and sincere in your approach to lovemaking and to your lover. Being sincere does not imply being serious, however. Seriousness comes from the mind, while sincerity arises from the heart. When we're being serious, we want a recipe for "do this, then do that," but the sincere lover allows for experimentation and playfulness. Like peeling an onion, layer after layer of your authentic core will be revealed as you relax.

Never judge yourself or your lover. Right and wrong are extraneous, and rules don't apply. Your body knows what to do! Your mind is superfluous here. That may be a strange or even frightening thought. We are all so used to being in control and making decisions and carrying them out. We are all so geared toward doing that we've forgotten how to just be. And yet being is natural. Being is what we do best! You'll be surprised at the wisdom you carry within when you relax and listen and feel and be. When that wisdom is allowed to guide you, it will lead you to unimaginable pleasure in lovemaking and indescribable joys in life.

PART TWO
The Keys to Spiritual Lovemaking

Introducing the Keys to Spiritual Lovemaking

The concept of *keys* is taken from Diana Richardson's book *The Heart of Tantric Sex: A Unique Guide to Love and Sexual Fulfillment.* I offer you these powerful keys in a way I hope will make them the most accessible and understandable for you, and Peter and I discuss them based on our personal experience with adopting them and internalizing their messages.

You can experiment with these nine keys one at a time, or you can incorporate any number of them into a single lovemaking session. Each will deepen your relaxation into sex and magnify the experience of lovemaking. They will bring you into a closer and deeper connection with your lover. Start with the keys that at first glance seem easiest to incorporate, but please don't deny yourself the opportunity to grow using the keys that seem least attractive or appropriate. I personally have been surprised and delighted by the joys given to me by the keys I was least inclined to try.

Sometimes what we fear or suspect most is actually what will open us up the most and expand us into the most intense pleasure.

On first reading, you may feel you've already used some of these keys or even that they are already part of your habitual lovemaking. If that is the case, please take a second look and try to consciously use these keys in new and different ways—in relaxed ways. I think you'll find them fresh and new and even revolutionary for you. Let these keys open the door to relaxed sex for you. Let them open the door to a conscious, amplified connection with your partner and with your spirit.

KEY ONE

Relaxation

Relaxation is the process of becoming increasingly alive.
—*Diana Richardson*

Okay, let's settle in and relax here, because while we touched on the concept of relaxing in chapter 3, we're going to delve into much more detail now. This is perhaps the most important key, since relaxation is, in a very real sense, what spiritual sex is all about. In fact, you could even say that relaxation is what spirituality as a whole is all about.

In chapter 4, we mentioned the fact that we each have physical aspects (obviously, our physical bodies and everything physical in our earthly experience) and non-physical aspects (our thoughts, feelings, and emotions). This duality of being is what makes life so interesting. These two elements, when in sync and connected, allow us to live fully and to feel whole and vibrant in mind and body. It may not seem immediately obvious, but relaxation truly is key to this kind of connection to our non-physical selves and therefore to our perception of our world as benevolent, friendly, and carrying the potential for joy. Relaxation brings about alignment. Alignment of the physical and non-physical makes lovemaking a truly spiritual event.

Many books have been written about this connection to the non-physical and the importance of thought and emotion in the shaping of our lives. Some books deal with thinking your way to success and riches. Others are about feeling your way into better relationships, and we've all certainly heard the phrase "be in touch with your feelings." This book is specifically about spiritual sex, however, so we're going to cut through all of the success-oriented dogma and talk about pure pleasure. We're going to think our way to "success at feeling great." We're going to feel our way to "success at simply being." And the magic? Once you've mastered relaxing into sex, you'll find that other avenues in your life will light up for you, and what previously seemed difficult or even impossible will suddenly appear before you in a natural unfolding.

How can I make such a gigantic claim? It's all in the relaxation. Once you can relax into sex, you can relax into life. And when you relax into life, you are connected. And when you are connected, you are whole, and anything is possible when your true personal power is available for you to use for whatever you like. In a relaxed and present state, you are ready for anything. You are inspired, energized, and able. And joy? Well, get ready.

By the time you've finished reading this chapter, I think you'll be on your way to being truly relaxed. The joy that was always there will reveal itself when you are relaxed.

You're probably asking yourself what I could possibly be going on about. How could relaxing possibly have all that power? After all, isn't relaxing just … doing *nothing*? How can we do nothing and get all that success and joy and good sex? Well, here's one of those places I warned about in my introduction where I repeat myself:

It's about connection. It's about easily and naturally re-solving any conflicts (even the ones you didn't know you had) between your physical and non-physical aspects. You're going to bring your thoughts and emotions right back to where they are integrated with your physical being. You're going to un-fragment your being so that you can feel whole and alive and completely present. *That* is relaxation. Presence. Being. Not doing.

Okay, I think you can agree with me there. Relaxation is "not doing." We're on the same page as long as I talk about nothing to do, no place to go, and no goal to accomplish. Or at least, you'll agree, relaxation is not doing something for any particular purpose. Perhaps you're thinking that going fishing could be relaxing, as could playing basketball. If you are a commercial fisherman with a quota or a professional basketball player, however, you might not relax so easily into the activity because you have specific goals to accomplish. Making love is exactly the same. Many of us no longer see lovemaking as an inspired and totally relaxed and sensual act, and have fallen into the trap of seeing it as just one more activity we can do well or not, succeed at or not, and so on.

Any activity that you do for sheer joy and inspiration can be relaxing. When you are engaged in something that you feel you almost can't "not do," or when you are so en-grossed in something that you forget the time and place— no matter what that activity may be—you are relaxed. You may never have thought of it this way, but even if you are doing something with fast and furious action and even if you are creating and accomplishing, if you have lost track of time and are in a state of doing for the sake of doing, then you are completely and profoundly *relaxed*!

You might think that this contradicts my earlier harping on the need to *be here now* and to have no goal or thought of accomplishment or endpoint in mind. There is no contradiction! Think of a time when you were inspired by a creative project—or even a chore—where you were so engrossed in what you were doing that you lost all concept of why you were doing it or what you were trying to get done. Think about that…and remember that, for the time you were "lost" in your activity, you were not thinking about the goal, but rather you were in the flow of *NOW*. And you were so present and *connected* and un-fragmented in mind and body that you fully gave yourself over to whatever you were doing, and the doing for its own sake became a source of joy. Focused, conscious relaxation became unbridled *joy*. I hope it was easy for you to remember a time when this was true for you. Recall when you came up for air and noticed that you had gotten a lot done, or you noticed that you had just had a ton of *fun*. You felt exhilarated, yes. And you also felt *relaxed*.

Inspiration is relaxing. Motivation is not.

Consider the difference between being inspired to do something and being motivated. Motivation comes from outside of you. It involves some kind of reward or fulfillment of an expectation for a specific reason. Inspiration comes from within. It bubbles up out of your connection with your authentic and whole self. Inspiration to action never feels difficult or daunting. Inspired action is freeing, joyful, easy, and fun.

Diana Richardson expresses it perfectly when she says that true relaxation is not a "checking out" but rather a "checking in." It's checking in with our inner, non-physical selves and allowing our being to take over our doing.

We've all been taught that to achieve our goals and aims in life, we need to have a plan and to execute the plan successfully. We produce effort and tension in order to see our plan through to completion. Somewhere along the line we lost the ability to break out of that mold and give ourselves the opportunity, at least in part of our lives, to live in a state of aimless and goal-less being.

Imagine you have a job where your boss requires you to create something, and he or she gives you parameters, endpoints, and deadlines. How easy is it to get inspired? How relaxed will you feel as you fulfill expectations and take actions specifically designed to get you to the required objective? You may enjoy your work, but you will enjoy it in tension, and you will take your satisfaction from a "job well done." There's nothing wrong with that. It's just not "relaxing into work."

Imagine instead that you have absolutely no employer, no thought of reward or payment, and no deadlines or outside expectations, but that you are full of creative ideas and have been given unlimited access to the time and resources to bring your ideas to fruition. You can simply follow your impulses and create whatever and however you please, with complete freedom and abandon and the absolute guarantee that whatever you create will be pleasing. You don't even have to come up with an end product. You are free to play in whatever creative way moves your spirit, with no guidelines, no rules. Now, you can relax. You can integrate your own non-physical desires and thoughts and ideas with your physical body, your tools, your surroundings, and even with time and space—and off you go into action. Inspired action. Joyful action. Relaxed action.

I think you are beginning to understand. Relaxation is connection. It's authenticity.

In a relaxed state you may do things, but what you do springs joyfully from what you are. So the being comes first. Then the doing will take care of itself.

Relaxation for Spiritual Lovemaking

It's not a surprise that many of us have picked up the idea that we can make love in a right way or a wrong way, and that we can succeed or fail at it with respect to our partner's excitement and achievement of orgasm. No wonder we don't relax! Intuitively we know that lovemaking should be a refuge, a place of acceptance and peace. We all long for that. Yet how many of us actually experience it that way? How many of us can turn off our habitual striving when we approach the sex act? After all, there are goals here as well! First, orgasm—it's a given we're shooting for that. And then there are better orgasms, and simultaneous orgasms, and on and on. We've made sex into a good-better-best game, and relaxing has certainly taken a back seat, if it's an element at all.

Well, now you are learning to *relax into sex*, and this will make all the difference. We've already talked about taking the goal of orgasm out of the equation and just allowing our beings to enjoy themselves unhindered by outcome. Now let's delve more deeply into the relaxation itself. Let's get even more closely connected to ourselves and allow even more profound focus and consciousness as we allow ourselves to *be here now*.

Peter's favorite line from Diana Richardson's *The Heart of Tantric Sex* is:

**Relaxation is the process of
becoming increasingly alive.**

Read that sentence a few times and allow it to sink in. It's quite a profound concept, and it's the heart of what we are teaching here. Relaxation is not a cessation of life, it's not taking a break from life, and it's not turning off. Rather, it's the process of becoming even more alive and vital.

A relaxed being is not a weak being. When you relax, you do not release your life force. When you relax, you do not collapse into yourself and release your vitality. When you relax, you are not depleted or deflated. In fact, it's quite the opposite. As you allow the integration of your physical and non-physical aspects, you become inflated with vitality. True relaxation is the feeling of being alive, with no pressure, no expectations, and no effort. It is life for life's own sake. It is energy, with no need to be artificially energetic.

Be aware that this true relaxation demands your conscious focus. You must choose to relax. Choose to connect. Choose to bring yourself into alignment with all of the elements of yourself and be profoundly present in this moment. You are probably out of practice, so at first as you make this choice, it may almost feel like an effort not to collapse into yourself and simply "check out." So remember, checking out is not relaxation. Checking out is *not* being here now. Allow yourself to make the choice. When you try this again and again, purposefully, your being will soon come to recognize and gravitate toward the letting go more easily and quickly.

Be here now.

How to Relax

First, you have to agree that relaxation has some merit, and you must consciously decide that you're going to engage in some (real) relaxation. I point this out because your powerful mind can play tricks on you. You might go through the motions of what you're reading here, but if your mind is still trapped in the groove of your previous belief that relaxation has to be earned or that relaxation comes *after* sex, not during, or that relaxation can't really and truly be of any benefit, then your efforts to relax might be wasted.

So read over the first part of this key several times and check in with your previous beliefs. Acknowledge that we're onto something a little different here, and that you're making a choice to be inspired by your nature, rather than motivated by those beliefs that no longer serve you. Don't worry if it takes time and a little bit of two steps forward and one step back. You will make the shift in understanding that relaxing is beneficial to every aspect of your life. And as you make the shift, you'll enjoy every step of the journey.

During sex, resolve to do less and be more. This may be challenging at first, because habits can keep a strong hold. Be gentle with yourself. Focus inward. Remember that by relaxing, you will not be collapsing inward but rather gathering life force and vitality. Focus on each body part in succession. Ask yourself where you are holding tension. Ask your shoulders, your knees, your neck, your feet... travel around your body and focus on any feeling of blocked energy or tension, and consciously let go. Then... let go again. You'll be amazed at how many layers of tension can be accessed as you do this exercise over and over again in one session.

After you have checked in with your extremities, focus on your pelvic floor, and release any tension there. The jaw is associated with the anal and pelvic areas, so as you relax, release your jaw muscles as well. Gently form the sound "ah" while letting the muscles of your face slacken.

Tune in to your solar plexus—that soft hollow point in the center of your chest, just below your ribs. Most of us do not have a conscious awareness of the energy in that area on a regular basis. Bringing your awareness to your solar plexus can be very powerful, and it's worth your attention. The solar plexus is an emotional center, and the feelings stored there, when allowed to flow, will grant you access to deeper relaxation.

We all have the ability to relax deeply. You may think of yourself as a fidgety or wired person and want to say, "I can't relax. It's just not in my nature." In fact, however, you do have the ability to relax, and for you the difference will be all the more profound and positive. By the same token, try not to judge your partner's level of relaxation. As you relax, you will affect the energy in your entire environment, and your partner will sense this and relax more easily. The woman, as she becomes more and more deeply relaxed, can focus on receptivity, openness, and sensitivity. The man, as he becomes more focused in the present moment and tension leaves his body, may release all thoughts of orgasm as he enjoys the experience of really feeling, perhaps for the first time, all of the nuances available in lovemaking. Without tension, there is ever so much more feeling. Without tension, an entire world of sensation is available.

Don't worry if, as you relax, your body responds with a desire to fall asleep. This is natural, especially when the muscles have been held in tension for some time without your awareness. Use your deliberate focus to ask each body part how it is feeling and whether there is yet another layer of tension that might be released. As you stay present and aware, your desire to drift into sleep will dissipate, and you will feel ever more alive even as you relax more and more deeply.

Give yourselves plenty of time. Relaxation, while naturally available, can take time to perfect as an art in lovemaking. To avail yourself of the magic of relaxation, it's best to set aside several hours where nothing is expected of you and you expect nothing of yourself, except pleasure.

All you have to do is make love.

Have fun. Be playful. Touch. Look. Be present.

In relaxed sex, making love entails far less physical effort and far more awareness and presence. When you emerge from a lovemaking session that is truly relaxed, whether you have experienced orgasm or not, you will bring a shimmering quality to the rest of your activities. Your entire life will be infused with a joyful, loving, and authentic energy.

KEY TWO

Your Breath

Life is like sex. If you want a happy ending, don't rush.
—Paulo Coelho

Breathe in. Breathe out. You probably think you've had that one down for a while now. Yes, I know you've been doing this since the first moment you made your appearance on the planet, and yes, it's true that breathing is usually involuntary. It's not usually something you have to control. After all, if you had to be focused and aware every time you drew in a breath, you'd have absolutely no time for anything else. Breathing is something you do while you do anything and everything else. It rarely stands on its own as an isolated and complete activity. Asking you to be aware of your breathing may seem akin to asking you to be aware of your heart beating.

The word *spirit* derives from the Latin *spiritus*, which means "breath."

Yet as basic as breathing is, and however many years you've already practiced this skill, I promise you that there are infinite layers to and nuances of breathing that have escaped you until this moment. By mastering, or even just experimenting with, the key of breath, you'll take your sexual experience to new heights of possibilities. Worth a try, isn't it?

Breathing awakens sexual feeling, and it activates our sexual energy. Like all of what this book teaches, conscious breathing brings about awareness of self and of the here and

now. Focused breathing brings even more exquisite awareness of all of your body's sensations, not just of the parts
between your nose and your belly.

Most of us think of foreplay as anything that comes before penetration. We are usually focused on "touch here,
touch there"—lots of doing and very little being. Try a new
way of using the minutes before lovemaking by including
focused breathing. It will slow you down, bring you into
the present moment, and awaken your senses. If you do this
kind of relaxed breathing by yourself, even before your lover
arrives, he or she will feel your heightened sensitivity and
aliveness as soon as you come together. You'll feel grounded
and ready to receive your lover, not scattered and in need of
touching to bring you to the here and now.

Even if you are a master at meditation and have spent
countless hours focused on your breath, you'll find that
using the breath to help you relax into sex brings an even
deeper and more fulfilling dimension to that practice.

Breathe in. Breathe out. Bring what is usually unconscious into your fully conscious awareness. Focus only on
the breath. In. Out. Slowly and rhythmically.

As you breathe in and out in this focused way, you'll
notice that you need to stop pretty much everything else
you're doing (perhaps even reading this) and give your full
awareness and attention to breathing. Just breathing. Nothing else. In. Hold a few seconds. Out. In. Expand. Expand a
little more. Then relax. Breathe through your nose or your
mouth, whichever feels most comfortable to you. Or al-

ternate. It doesn't matter. What matters is your conscious awareness of your breath. It is you, being here, now, and focused on bringing life to every cell of your body, empowering them, vitalizing them, and relaxing them.

Deep Rhythmic Breathing

As you read this, take a breath in. As you inhale, pay attention to the breath's final destination. Does it stop not much lower than your throat? Does your chest rise? Do you feel your solar plexus area expand? What about your belly? If you are like most people and have spent very little time paying conscious attention to what your inhalations are doing and where they are going, and if you are an adult in modern Western society, then you are likely to have found that the breath you just took stopped somewhere around nipple level.

If you saw anything expand, it was probably your chest area. That's okay. Breathe in again. This time, consciously try to push your breath deeper into your body. Breathe in slowly. As you breathe, open your belly. Relax the front of your body and attempt to expand outward. Fill your belly-balloon with air. Expand that balloon as far as you can. Then, when it feels full to capacity and wants release, exhale slowly, in a relaxed exhalation, letting the belly slowly deflate again. You've just given your body a grand injection of life-giving oxygen. Yes, I know you were not dying before this exercise, but having taken that one expanding and relaxing breath, you are more alive now! I promise.

Every single time you allow yourself to stop, pay attention, and breathe in this manner—pushing the air in, taking it into you as deeply as you can in as much volume as you can, followed by a relaxed and full exhalation—you enliven yourself all the more. The depth of the breath you take changes everything. As you practice the skill of expanding yourself outward with every breath, you will begin to take in more oxygen even during times when you necessarily give over your focus to other things. It will become an unconscious habit to breathe in fully and deeply.

A conscious habit of deep breathing awakens your sex center. An unconscious habit of shallow breathing is actually a habit that causes less sexual energy to circulate in the body. In chapter 1, we said that sexual energy is the life force, the very vital force that informs everything we do. Breathing facilitates the circulation of that energy all the more. When you inhale deeply, the energy is brought all the way down to your genitals. Try to inhale so deeply that you can actually feel your genital area awakening as you breathe.

Men sometimes report that even though they've previously been unable to attain or sustain strong erections, when they practice deep, focused breathing, this problem disappears. Likewise, women who report dryness in the vagina or painful intercourse become naturally open and moist after a session of deep, sustained breathing into the belly and down into the genitals.

Focused Breathing

Inhale. Bring the energy into your body. Expand and push down. Exhale. Release the energy, allowing it to circle back. As the cycle completes, repeat it slowly and consciously. Try to exhale completely. Empty your belly and your lungs. Allow the energy complete release and freedom. As you release the breath, you relax. And as you relax, you become one with the present moment. You are here. Now.

Make it a point to inhale deeply as you and your partner start to make love. Then focus on exhaling fully. Give yourself over completely to experiencing lovemaking with your partner. Receive energy. Release energy. Deeply. Completely. Breathe in, breathe out. Deeply, completely. Surrender to the experience you are having in the here and now. Complete exhalation ensures that you relax, and complete inhalation ensures that you are energized. Both are vitally important for the fullest realization of ecstasy.

Use your imagination as you breathe deeply. Imagine that as you inhale all the way down to your sex center, you are taking in your partner. Receive him or her completely, with no reservations. As you exhale, imagine you are releasing your partner, gently, completely, into relaxed freedom. In. Out. Focus on the depth of your inhalation and the completeness of your exhalation.

Breathing in Rhythm and Sync

Now that you have the hang of being consciously aware of your breath, you can use this skill for some interesting experiences during lovemaking. After you focus for a time on your own relaxation and breath, you may notice that you and your lover have fallen into a synchronous pattern of breathing. Perhaps you are breathing in rhythm. You both breathe in … then out, at the same time; the length and depth of your breaths are identical, as if you are one body reacting to the same intention to bring the energy in and then release it, over and over again. If you notice this happening, enjoy it. Bring your attention to it. You can try to prolong this phenomenon as long as it feels natural and relaxed. Never try to push this or any other action in sex, as any effort involved will dampen the benefits of this wonderful occurrence. If you fall out of rhythm, go back to focusing on your own relaxed breathing.

Sometimes you'll find your lover breathing out just as you breathe in, and vice versa. This, too, can be relaxing and connecting, as you softly bring your awareness to this and allow it to continue without effort or resistance. It's always more important to breathe in your own natural rhythm than to synchronize your breathing, although this can feel wonderful when it happens.

If you feel yourself drawn outside the present moment at any time during lovemaking, use deep, slow, conscious breathing to bring yourself back to the here and now. If you find yourself becoming very excited during sex, you may notice that your breath is becoming shorter and faster. To relax back into full body awareness, release the sexual energy from concentration in the genitals by consciously slowing down the rhythm of your breathing. This will encourage the body to absorb the sexual energy rather than release it. This is a powerful tool for relaxing and prolonging your lovemaking. When lovers breathe rhythmically, deeply, and slowly, ejaculation and/or orgasm are unlikely to occur.

Peter:
Like all the techniques we cover in this book, deep, rhythmic, conscious breathing will have a positive effect on your entire life—not just your sex life. I do not exaggerate at all when I say that by becoming consciously aware of my breathing in the midst of everyday situations, my life has changed dramatically.

Breathing and relaxing are inextricably linked. It is impossible to stay tense and stressed if you are conscious of your breathing and you are making a concerted effort to breathe deeply and slowly. For example, if I am in the midst of a disagreement with someone, the mere fact that I have learned to focus on my breath—even for a moment—always results in my noticing that my breathing is shorter and faster than it needs to be, and in that noticing I begin to relax. I watch my breath—it takes only a few seconds—and the situation always becomes smoother.

With lovemaking in particular, as you ride the hills and valleys of a relaxed sexual romp, deep, slow breathing allows your bodies to better mold to each other, and you feel an increased vitality flowing through your entire body—including your genitals.

In lovemaking, as men we tend to be "ready" long before our female counterpart, and for many men this can result in ejaculation long before either one of you really wants it to happen. I personally have found that by regulating my breath to a slow and easy rhythm, I can actually feel the tension leaving my body, and at the same time, the energy flow to my genitals makes me feel both stronger and calmer. Typically, as you become more excited and find yourself heading toward release, slowing down your breathing pattern can help you settle into a groove that can literally last for hours.

There are times when Jody and I tune in to each other's breath, at times falling naturally into breathing in unison, and sometimes the opposite. When one of us feels sleepy but wants to stay alert and involved in lovemaking, by focusing on our breath, we come back more firmly into the moment and engage with our own body, and that of the other. It is like a language you begin speaking to each other, a wordless language of ocean waves of breath, rising and falling. Try it when your genitals and mouths are locked together and your chests are moving in unison.

Another magical use of the breath (Jody regularly requests this) is to gently breathe on the back of your lover's neck. While spooning behind your partner, place your lips almost imperceptibly between her shoulders or just beneath her hairline. Make sure you are both comfortable, perhaps with a pillow between your knees, and simply hold your lover and breathe slow and easy such that your warm breath stimulates those tiny little hairs along her spine. Your breath is almost a subtle penetration, and its rhythm can carry you both along for hours.

Breathing is an easy key to practice, in or out of the bedroom. You will soon find yourself consciously breathing long, delicious breaths in any and all situations—in a checkout line at a store, for example, or while sitting in a theater. Try watching and controlling your breath while driving on an easy stretch of road. Slower, deeper breathing means less tension, more alertness, and a more satisfying experience, whatever you may be doing in the moment.

KEY THREE

Touch

*Wherever two lovers' energies are meeting and mingling,
there is life, alive, at its best.*
—Osho

It's natural for us to crave the touch of another. We all love to be touched.

Perhaps you are nodding your head in agreement, even sighing a "yes!" Or maybe you are thinking, "No, not me! I don't like to be touched. I need my space." If you are in the latter group, you might agree that under the right circumstances, when you feel comfortable and it is appropriate, you adore the feeling of touching and being touched. This is a natural human need and tendency, and we risk damaging ourselves if we try to deny it. Touch, sexual or otherwise, is as natural as breathing, if we allow ourselves to relax into it.

While some of us are more touchy-feely and receptive to touch than others, we all share a natural state of being that is open to and even needs the touch of our fellow human beings. In some societies, even today, entire families sleep together, so loving, nonsexual touch happens every day. Psychologists and sociologists have often noted that children raised in families that touch a lot are the most successful, emotionally stable, and secure. It serves us to remember that our natural tendency is to want to touch one another and not to keep distance and physical barriers between our bodies.

Since this is a book about sex, you knew touching would be involved, of course, but this key is not about the kind of touch that is applied for stimulating or being stimulated, or even the affectionate touch we are accustomed to thinking of in connection with lovemaking. Rather, it's about a whole new world of *relaxed* touch. It's a whole new world of *conscious* touch.

Wherever you are on the continuum of "like to be touched" versus "can't stand to be touched," you can learn to relax into sex with a partner you love and trust. Using the key of touch, you will enhance not only your lovemaking but your entire life as well.

I'm not saying we're about to turn you into someone who will show up at the office tomorrow and rush to hug your boss when you say good morning. I am saying, however, that by relaxing into sex and tuning in to your natural ability to focus on the feeling of touching and being touched, you'll feel refreshed and energized and different— yes, even by tomorrow morning!

Most of us have learned to touch our partners as an "action." Touch starts with a thought, and with an objective in mind, albeit a lovely objective: to feel or cause pleasure. We touch with purpose and hope we are "doing it right." Relaxed sex, however, is about touching as a form of allowing your natural body intelligence to take over. It's about releasing thought and allowing focused awareness instead.

Since you've read this far, you won't be surprised to know that the point of this key—like all the keys, and relaxed sex as a whole—is to *be here now*, and to be fully present in the moment. The key of touch, perhaps more than any of the keys we've talked about till now, will ground you right here, with your lover, in the present experience. Relaxing into touch is another way of applying conscious awareness and being truly present.

Relaxed Touch

Lying next to your lover and using the other keys—you are taking deep, energizing, and cleansing breaths, you are taking one another in with your eyes, and you are infusing your genitals with awareness—you now take that same awareness and make your touch come alive. Your skin becomes the vehicle for focusing and transmitting your sexual energy, your life force energy.

Start with a little space between the two of you. Just sense your partner's body before you reach for it. Feel the electricity in the space you are holding. Now focus that electricity into your hand . . . and . . . touch.

You can start anywhere, but there are several areas of the body that are particularly sensitive and conducive to the use of this key, especially as you start out. Try placing your hand on your lover's sacrum (the part of the lower back that joins with the buttocks). An open palm or gentle massage there sends radiating sensations of warmth to the rest of the body. The back of the neck, when held softly by the entire hand, provides a feeling of security and a safe release of emotion. Tears may flow easily as a result of being touched here. For women, gentle massage of the legs and buttocks can sometimes serve to release pent-up sexual energy that rests there.

As you touch your partner, run your hand over their body while focusing your awareness into that hand. As you relax into this activity, you might become aware that over the years you've developed certain habits of touch. Perhaps some ideas of what kinds of touch feel good to your partner have become ingrained and never questioned. You've probably followed a touching sequence that has become close to second nature. First touch here, then there … whatever has worked for you in the past. Now is your opportunity to expand those beliefs and patterns and perhaps change them as you learn, as if for the first time, what it is like to touch a lover's body and to be touched in return when you are fully aware and conscious of every sensation.

Be curious. Experiment, all the while keeping your awareness focused, not on what is coming next but on what you are feeling now—right now—as you touch. Imagine your hand as a warm vessel gently pouring love and energy everywhere it roams on your partner's skin. Try to just *be* as you touch. Rather than thinking of touch as an action, think of it as a state of being. Stop and hold your connection now and then. Rest quietly in the experience of skin touching. Then slowly begin again.

Now that you've tried some of the other keys and understand that the purpose of relaxed sex is not the goal of orgasm, and now that you've learned to set aside plenty of time for lovemaking, you can begin to use your touch in an entirely new way. Stroke curiously and slowly, allowing yourself to be surprised when even the most familiar part-

ner's body shows itself to you as something new and different and infinitely lovely. Touching is a subtle yet powerful
form of communication. You may use the key of voice communication while you touch, but also allow for periods of
silence. Allow touch to show its true power when it is used
alone. Conscious touching can form a bond that informs all
of the other keys, if you give it the time and focus it needs
to work its magic.

Rather than think to yourself, "I'm now stroking my partner's body," try to become even more finely tuned, and ask
yourself how the contours of your partner's body feel; follow
their lines and curves and hollows, and tune in to the sensation of your hand. Even if you've touched this body a thou-
sand times before, as you bring conscious awareness to your
touch and you slow down, you'll be amazed at the discoveries
at your fingertips.

Touch with focus and consciousness ... slowly and deliberately. Infuse your touch with love and warmth, and imagine you are infusing your lover with these qualities with
each feathery or firm contact.

I repeat the words *focus* and *consciousness* because they
are indeed the keys to this key, if you will. You may usually
be affectionate and gentle, and perhaps you often use touch
as foreplay to feel your lover's body and to make him or her
feel good as well. When you relax into sex, however, you are
doing so much more. By focusing your consciousness into
your touch, you are magnifying its effect one hundredfold!
The exact same stroking or touching or caressing will feel

so much better and have so much more meaning when it is done with focused awareness. You will feel the difference, and your partner will feel the difference.

Nothing compares with being touched by a lover whose entire being is focused on touching you in that moment. The presence of love is so very much more profound when awareness is concentrated into the moment, into the now, and, in the case of touch, into the *here*. When your lover touches you with awareness, you feel truly touched. When your lover touches you with awareness, you feel truly loved. And likewise, when you touch with awareness, you summon your own ability to be a conduit for energy and love. It is a two-way street, or more accurately, a circle, of energy and love.

Massage can be a wonderful beginning to a lovemaking session. Most of us accept massage as touch with no particular goal in mind except relaxation, so it can be a great segue into lovemaking. With massage, typically one partner gives and the other receives. Whether you give or receive, bring your awareness fully to touching or to being touched. Empty your mind of all thoughts, and focus on the feeling, the sensation, in its every nuance, of touching or being touched. What does your hand feel like? What temperature is it—is it radiating pulsing warmth or fresh coolness? How smooth or rough is your partner's skin? Where are the hills and valleys along the contours of your lover's body? Is your touch gentle and caressing, or is it firm and vigorous? Touch or allow yourself to be touched, with no goal in mind, with no thought of excitement or titillation. Focus softly on the touch itself and the subtle electric current that it causes to flow between you, back and forth in a circuit of energy.

Don't be fooled by the seeming simplicity of this key. While certainly you have always touched your lover and you have been touched in return, relaxing into sex is asking you to touch in a completely different way. Understanding the subtleties of this difference can give you an aha moment of great importance! The first time you really feel your hand come alive with electricity or you feel your body receive that electrical impulse while being touched by your partner, you will have transformed all future lovemaking sessions. Practice this skill of focusing your awareness and energy into your hand or wherever you are touching your lover. Similar to genital awareness, this focused awareness of touch carries amazing power.

And don't forget about polarity.

The woman's positive pole, her breasts and heart area, are exquisitely sensitive to focused, aware touch. When time is spent on lovingly touching the breasts, the woman's entire body becomes infused with energy.

If you are a woman accustomed to a man touching your breasts more as a means to become excited than to deliver loving warmth to you, then perhaps you have not allowed yourself to fully appreciate the power of the positive pole. Over the years, you may have begun to deny the power of the breasts and the positive heart pole. In relaxed sex, you will have an opportunity to slow down and tune your own awareness to being touched on your breasts, and in short order you may find your attitudes changing and your body receiving that touch more openly and joyfully.

If you are a man who believed he had to give attention to the breasts and nipples in order to "turn on" his woman, then you too will be amazed at how this key to relaxed sex can open up a new world of sensation when touching the breasts with awareness, love, and focus. Start over as if you've never touched a woman's breasts before. Infuse your hand with energy, and relax into caressing and loving the breasts.

The same applies to the man's positive pole, his penis. While touching and being touched there, keep your awareness on local sensation and the flow of energy. Explore slowly, gently, and with consciousness.

Focus on every nuance and every contour, fold, and crevice in the body, one by one.

Slow down. Be here now. Touch. Be touched. Note the difference.

As you move your touch to include every part of each other's body, slowly and consciously your bodies and hearts will respond in ways you have never experienced before. Will you be sexually excited? Very likely you will … but you'll also experience yourself and your lover in a much more highly charged and energetic way. You'll come to know each other more deeply, and love and appreciation will grow exponentially.

As in meditation, you might find your mind wandering and realize you've been touching your partner—or your partner has been touching you—but your awareness has been focused elsewhere. When this happens, gently refocus your awareness and go back to fully experiencing the touch. This is a skill that takes practice, but the results are so worthwhile. Over and over, gently and with understanding, bring your focus back firmly to the here and now and to what you are feeling and doing.

Remember, this is a different kind of touch than what you have probably been accustomed to. I repeat this because it is vitally important to remember that we are not simply saying, like many books and articles you've probably read before, "touch here, then there." Instead, the message of relaxed sex is "touch with awareness" here, then there...and anywhere! Touch with awareness. Touch with energy. Touch with focus. Not with purpose.

Focus. Touch. Bring your focus in again. Touch. Slowly. Keep your awareness right here. Right now. Don't go away in thought. Don't plan where your hand or any other body part will go next. Just touch. Be aware. Focus. Touch.

Peter:

For many men like myself, and perhaps some women, too, the sex act is one of the few times we allow ourselves to experience really feeling another person's body—the aliveness, and the energy. I have never been much of a toucher. Physical affection outside of sex did not come naturally to me. My father always shook my hand, and never really hugged me or my brothers. In adulthood, I took it upon myself to cultivate a very affectionate and loving relationship with my mother, including a hello and goodbye kiss and hug. After a while, she followed my lead, but I had to make the conscious decision that physical affection would be part of my interactions with my mom, and it was awkward at first as I practiced it. In time, with Mom, as with Jody and others in my life, it came to feel more and more natural for me to reach out with a touch, a hug, or a kiss. I've often envied those who were raised in more physically demonstrative cultures.

The following exercise is something that's helped me develop an ability that did not come naturally. This exercise at first glance may seem simple or even silly, but don't underestimate its power. It really will give you a good illustration of what can be accomplished with relaxed, goalless, fully conscious touch.

An Exercise in Touch

When you are alone and have some quiet time, sit or lie down comfortably. It is best to try this exercise first in silence, but you could add some meditative music, if you'd like. You can close your eyes if it helps you to focus. Place the fingers of one hand ever so gently across your own forehead, right up along your hairline. As you move along, shift your consciousness back and forth between the feeling in your fingertips and the feeling in your forehead. Shift your focus between being touching and being touched. Try to feel only one of these sensations at a time.

Very, very slowly, begin moving your hand down your face, but take lots of time to really feel the contours of your face. Feel your forehead—its texture and topography. Feel your eyebrows. Run your fingers along them. Remember to be both the toucher and the touchee, gently alternating, back and forth. Giving and taking, at the same time. There are some mental gymnastics involved here!

Let your fingers slowly make their way over the slopes of your eyelids. Touch your eyelashes. As you continue down your face, taking your time and always switching back and forth, describe for yourself (even out loud) how it feels to be touched, to touch, each tiny area. I find it easier to imagine receiving the touch. Being the one doing the touching requires me to somehow switch myself around in a way that is a little trickier to maintain. It's an interesting challenge, and well worth the effort.

Continue over your chin, neck, lower throat, and chest. It's okay to compliment yourself on the magic in your hands. Try different degrees of firmness to your touch and caress. If you feel your mind wandering away from focusing on the exercise, you can always gently bring yourself back.

Try this exercise for just a minute at first. Each time you do this exercise, try to add another minute. You'll find it easier and easier to maintain your intention for longer periods, and soon your lover will be reaping the benefits of your ability to receive and give touch with intense focus and enjoyment.

Peter:

Waking up in a fine hotel in Sedona, Arizona, Jody and I opened the drapes and looked through the full-length windows overlooking a lush park with a thick snowfall on the ground, and more coming down in fat, moist flakes. No place to go. Nothing to do. Nothing to be. And room service. We took the opportunity to find out that touching can go on for hours, and far from becoming boring or repetitive, it can be something akin to playing sweet music together. The enjoyment seemed to go on endlessly. Only a sustenance or bathroom break interrupted the symphony.

That snowy day, with our needs satisfied in every way, was the perfect time for us to be introduced to the idea of touch as a relaxed, erotic art form, and we were lucky enough to have time standing still for us at that particular point in our lives. But even if your time with your lover is brief some days, you will benefit from taking just thirty full seconds of time to simply lean into your partner's most intimate personal space, place your cheeks against each other, and touch one another's face. As far as I am concerned, if you've done this with full focus and conscious awareness, you have just completed a Tantric sex session. In those thirty seconds of conscious touch, you will feel yourself rebalance and relax.

If you have a longer session of sensual touching, when you *do* finally allow the symphony to conclude (and I don't mean orgasm), you will walk away with an aliveness that is beyond compare. People can actually *see* it on you. Have you ever looked at one of your friends, and it is immediately obvious that he has some good news to tell you, even though he may be trying to act nonchalant? You can feel it in his energy, and you'll say something like, "You're in a particularly good mood today" or "What's up with you with that little smile?" *That* is how you feel after using your fingers, lips, arms, chest, hips, legs, and feet to touch your partner in a long, languid session. You will continue through your day with a somewhat angelic smile on your face. Relaxed sex, indeed.

So lie down with your partner for some designated "touch" sessions. These are times—short or long—when you both know you're probably not going to make love, but you just want to connect and touch. After just minutes of this, you will feel yourself relax and recharge, and the rest of the day will have an energetic calmness to it. Everything is in the touch. When we use touch to purposefully link to our partner, our whole world relaxes a little more.

KEY FOUR
Eye Contact

We don't see things as they are. We see them as we are.
—From the Talmud

Open your eyes!

Well, you may be thinking, that seems simple enough—I usually have my eyes open.

And perhaps you do. I thought I did. Except when I didn't! I found out that opening my eyes when anything intense was going on in my body was difficult and did not come naturally. My first instinct was actually to keep my eyes tightly closed during sex. I did not resist opening my eyes out of wanting not to see; rather, I closed my eyes instinctively because I did not want to be seen! It was only when I decided to intentionally keep my eyes open past my comfort zone that I came to understand this. I hadn't realized how much I had tried to keep hidden by closing my eyes, as if by not opening the windows to my being, I could keep myself safe and free from judgment.

This realization was important in that it gave me an opening to become truly free rather than to escape into the illusion of freedom. It meant I now had the choice to consciously allow myself to be exposed and known. Making the conscious choice to be present by keeping my eyes open more than usual during lovemaking caused all kinds of hell to break loose at first. I giggled. I laughed. I even cried. I averted my eyes to look at the ceiling, the clock... My eyes seemed to close of their own accord and had to be trained to let in the experience visually. It was well worth the effort, however, and had I not made it, many layers of sexual and personal connection would have eluded me forever. With deliberate practice, keeping my eyes open and making eye contact became second nature in a short time, and I forgot the old desire to retreat and hide.

It's natural to feel unsure when first practicing conscious eye contact with your lover. You may feel you won't measure up in some way, and that without the cover of action, your simple energetic, loving, and relaxed presence won't be enough.

Eye contact reveals you in your authenticity.

We instinctively know that we cannot hide anything with open eyes. It's tempting to close the eyes and take refuge in the actions and movements of our bodies, thinking, "I know what to do that will make me a good lover." When we are focused on *doing*, on performing actions that will excite our partner, vision isn't really necessary. This, however, denies your lover the opportunity to make love to *you* rather than with your body's actions.

Constantly closing the eyes isolates and divides. Unless you open your eyes to take in your lover and allow your lover's energy its entrance, you are making love essentially alone. You may be able to give and receive sexual excitement, but you will absent yourself from much of the experience.

Conscious Eye Contact

When you look softly at your partner's eyes, taking him or her in and allowing yourself to be taken in, you will feel a surge of sexual energy emitted from and into the eyes. Don't force yourself to stare without blinking, as this will cause distance rather than closeness. Take your lover into your sight softly, gently. Allow yourself to close your eyes and rest if you feel burning or dryness, as these indicate tension.

Opening your eyes and allowing full use of your sense of sight in lovemaking literally opens you to a fullness of sensation not possible when vision isn't employed. When we are conscious and aware of our own sensations and we have let go into *being*, opening the eyes allows a further sinking into the *now* and an even deeper immersion into awareness of the present moment.

You are here now. Your lover is here now.

Eye contact greatly increases the intimacy of lovemaking. You may be thinking that nothing could be more intimate than penis in vagina. And yet, with the added dimension of eye contact, seeing and being seen, the connection deepens. Allow yourself to gaze into your lover's eyes just past the point when you would normally break your gaze. Look. Feel. Be. Relax.

Try not to make seeing an action in and of itself. Rather, allow yourself to relax into vision. Relax and allow your eyes to focus in soft vision, gently taking in your lover, your surroundings, yourself.

Surprisingly, sustaining eye contact can take practice. You may find yourselves feeling self-conscious, and you might even burst into laughter or tears. Allow these feelings!

When opening your eyes feels really uncomfortable, allow yourself to close them for a time.

Making eye contact demands that a certain amount of space be held between lovers. In this space, the electric sexual energy can sizzle and polarity can be activated. Alternate between close embracing (which does not allow eye contact) and holding the space.

The simple key of opening your eyes and letting your lover in brings great benefits and deepened enjoyment of sex. The day will come when you'll look into your lover's eyes and feel an instant connection, a primal memory and recognition deep within.

Anyone who has ever experienced looking deep into the eyes of an animal, say a dog or a cat, knows that there can be true connection through focused eye contact. There can be communication. And there can most certainly be a tangible exchange of love energy. Energy exchange through the eyes can be extremely powerful, if you allow it. As with all avenues of personal energy exchange, we have the power to put up barriers, and more often than not, we do. It takes a conscious decision and intention to allow the eyes to—literally—open to your partner and let the energy and communication flow.

With strangers, eye contact can sometimes be incredibly uncomfortable. Anyone who has spent a minute or two crammed into an elevator knows that even if you are forced to face each other at close quarters, a short glance at each other is all that you are "allowed" to take. Then the connection must be broken. In fact, on those rare occasions when you make true eye contact with a stranger—say a waiter or a cashier—even though the moment is brief, the feeling it leaves you with can be quite lasting and profound.

You can, however, be in that very same crammed elevator, and, if there is a love connection between you and the person across from you, all those regular unseen social rules involving time and distance are relaxed or even dropped completely, depending on the level of your love connection with each other.

It's interesting to note that in a 1989 study by Kellerman, Lewis, and Laird in the *Journal of Research in Personality*, two opposite-sex strangers were asked to gaze into each other's eyes for two minutes, and in many cases that was enough to produce passionate feelings for each other! In many places, the idea of "speed dating"—where couples sit together for a very short period of time and ask each other a few questions—is being replaced by "eye gazing" sessions. Instead of questioning each other, dates look each other deeply in the eyes for a few long minutes. Many feel that this gives a deeper and truer picture of the other right away.

Peter:

I find it of great value to periodically look myself deeply in the eyes. That is to say, once in a while, instead of just looking in the mirror to wash, shave, or brush my teeth, I will take a real moment to stop, breathe, and look very closely at the man in the mirror. Sometimes I will lean in extra close to really lock on to my own gaze. Great mysteries can be revealed. There is no lying to the eyes, or through the eyes. And interestingly enough, gazing at yourself is a great warm-up for long, slow, meaningful gazing into your lover's eyes.

The idea that eye contact would be a helpful tool in lovemaking seems to be obvious enough. As males, we may sometimes be inclined to simply tick it off our list. (Look in her eyes. Okay, did that. Next.) But I'm not talking about just a glance or two during sex. I'm talking about prolonged, penetrating eye contact that reveals the deeper mysteries that lie just below the surface.

Eye contact will take you on an interesting emotional journey. As you gaze at each other, holding that gaze for several beats or more beyond the point where one of you would feel more comfortable turning away, you may pass through feelings of euphoria, sadness, laughter, and great calm. As best as you can, try to surrender to the experience. It can be rich and rewarding. Don't let an outburst of laughter cause you to halt the eye contact. Stay with it, keep laughing, and wait for the next wave of emotion to occur.

Don't be alarmed by the interesting phenomenon of morphing faces! After some time, your partner's face may seem to soften and morph into many different people. This isn't something happening to your partner, but is rather a reflection of your own inner processes and thoughts. If the image you see disturbs you in any way, gently turn your thoughts consciously to thoughts of love and affection, and you'll see your partner's face come into focus again as his or her own.

As Jody and I blissfully appreciate each other and everything we encounter, we talk constantly about the precepts and principles behind relaxed, spiritual lovemaking, and we put them into practice again and again. We have found that there is always a way to take things to the next level. When we decided to try some formal exercises to deepen our experience, we reasoned that we would benefit by challenging our comfort zones.

I thought we should start with an exercise involving what seemed like the easiest key to relaxed lovemaking, and I suggested we begin by exploring the world of deep and constant eye contact. Our connection was already so strong that I assumed eye contact between us would be a no-brainer.

Jody agreed in principle but was not as sure as I was that it would be easy. She had a strong intuition of exactly what was in store for us and how powerful it would be. When we were lying face to face with eyes open, I was surprised to discover that she found it hard to meet my gaze at first for more than a few nanoseconds! I gently persisted, however, and we reconfirmed for ourselves what a powerful tool this key really is.

Jody squirmed—both figuratively and literally—as we tried to "lock on" and maintain an unwavering visual connection. For me, too, it seemed more natural to let my gaze drift, to her lips, her hair, her entire face, returning only intermittently to her eyes. But we were both deter-mined to focus on the task at hand, so we continually coaxed each other to return to a steady, loving sharing of energy through our eyes.

And what happened? What happened was a profound dropping of barriers, a dropping of some sort of guard that we didn't even know we had set up. We didn't realize that we had previously allowed each other in just so far. With deep eye contact, we began to feel as if we were put-ting all the inconsequential things aside, and that we were really seeing right into the other's soul.

Be patient with yourself and your partner. Be aware that the benefits of this kind of eye-contact exercise do not make themselves known after a few seconds, or a few minutes. When you begin to get into the groove, your real, authentic self has no choice but to reveal itself, and energy begins to flow in earnest. When you soften yourself and open your own "windows to the soul," you not only let the other in, but you allow yourself to move into the other.

Eye contact is as intimate as it gets—as naked as it gets. The first time you try it, you will squirm like a basement dweller coming out into a sunny day. It will be that un-comfortable—especially for you big, strong, manly types. Be prepared to be stripped bare...then washed clean. And, as Jody discovered once she got past her "don't look at me" stage, then you will come to an entirely new level of affection and communication.

It turns out this "easy" exercise is a little like a balance-beam act. Constant adjustments and retries are in order, especially at first, until you find yourself in that quiet, effortless, steady, and comfortable place where all the darting and squirming and giggling have given way. You both will pass through a doorway and enter a cushy-furnished room where your spirits can really connect. When you combine this with being physically connected in love, eye contact becomes something unexpectedly profound and exhilarating.

An Exercise in Eye Contact

A really good way to ease into this practice is to start by gazing unwaveringly into your own eyes, in a mirror. See yourself as yourself. Allow yourself to open to yourself. See yourself as a vibrant, alive, sexual being. Basically, love yourself, through your own eyes.

Once you've tried this a few times on your own, it's time to move on to eye contact with your partner. I suggest that the very first time you try this, you may want to be in a comfortable, nonsexual situation, perhaps with both of you facing each other on the couch, fully dressed. Resist the temptation (and the escape) of reaching out and touching each other, as this will cause you to split your concentration. Simply project and receive love and affection from each other, solely through the eyes. Feelings of love will naturally rise to the surface, and the overall experience will be one of profound connection.

Can you practice deep eye contact only when you are feeling loving and affectionate toward your partner? No! In fact, it is at times of misunderstanding and negative emotion that it can sometimes do the most good. When you approach your partner through the eyes, it's almost inevitable that you will soften your heart and feel at one with your partner's being, so that if there is anger or resentment, it can turn into understanding, almost as if by magic.

Remember, this kind of prolonged eye contact is best done without words. Try it. It may be more difficult at first than you anticipate, but the rewards will be amazing and so worth it.

KEY FIVE

Voice Communication

*Words are also seeds, and when dropped
into the invisible spiritual substance,
they grow and bring forth after their kind.*
—Charles Fillmore

The secret to being truly alive is being here now. And using your voice to express the truth of your here and now is a very powerful key.

Communication became a hot topic in relationship psychology during the latter half of the twentieth century and continues to be talked about on a regular basis with respect to relationships. Psychologists and therapists of all disciplines teach couples talking skills in the belief that this will bring about understanding, and this understanding will facilitate closeness and harmony. There is, of course, much truth to this. However, studies over the same period of time demonstrate that over 75 percent (some say over 90 percent) of all human communication is nonverbal! This means that the greater part of our communication by far consists of bodily messages and behaviors, which we actually perform without conscious awareness of what we are communicating. So all that talk that has been and still is prescribed actually only scratches the surface of what we are getting across to our partners. And yet intuitively we do know that communicating is important. We want to communicate. We want to talk to one another. We want to bridge the distance. We crave closeness, and we want to be understood. So we talk and talk.

What's wrong with that?

Nothing... except that most of the talk is about anything but the here and now! It's usually about the past or the future—neither of which is actually being experienced as we talk. We might be rehashing something that we've experienced, either separately or as a couple. Sometimes we're even complaining in the past tense: "You did this..." and "That made me feel...."And let's face it, nobody, not even your therapist, can go back and change the past. Or we might be planning for the future, immediate or long-term. The problem with all of this so-called communication is that it's telling our partners what was or what will be, but almost never what *is*. It's explaining or requesting, but it's not describing who we *are* in the moment.

But relaxed sex offers you something even more powerful than understanding the past or planning for the future.

It offers you the present moment. It offers you the actual living of your life. The present is when you are experiencing your life, and it is when you are creating (not planning) your future. Now. *Now* is all you can possibly really experience! So *now* is all you can really communicate that will make a difference in the closeness you foster with your lover. *Now* is authentic. It's real. It makes no demands. It simply *is*.

Most of us rarely use our voices to communicate about this present moment, right here, right now. That can almost seem irrelevant and trivial. We believe that we can't enjoy the present until we've cleaned up or cleared up the past, or provided a plan for the future. After all, we are taught that if we unravel things that have already happened, or plan and plot what we would like to happen, then we are in control. Then we are "communicating."

By engaging in relaxed lovemaking, you are going to open up an entirely different mode of communication. It will be simple, although perhaps not easy at first. It still isn't very easy for me, but I've learned that the rewards are surprisingly great, and I hope you'll want to join me in trying to use this key. Each time you do, a deeper layer of authenticity will emerge—yours as well as your partner's. You will put yourself in touch with who you really are, and will allow your partner access to that authentic you. This feels amazingly good, and liberating. Just as with keys we've already discussed, the key of voice communication holds you in the present moment. It grounds you in the wonderful, magical *Here And Now*.

The secret to being truly alive is being here now, and using your voice to express the truth of your here and now is a very powerful key. Communication leads to true intimacy. When you don't let your partner know exactly what you are feeling, you actually block intimacy.

As you relax into sex, leave behind all of what you've thought words were for. Leave behind any effort to convince, request, recount, or explain. When you make love, you are, as always, communicating far more with your body and nonverbal expression than with your words, but here your words can have a profound effect on the sexual experience.

How?

You have probably read or heard somewhere that it's a good idea to communicate to your partner what you like during sex. You've been advised to show him or her where and how to touch you—usually with the purpose of increasing sexual excitement or moving you toward orgasm more quickly and efficiently. While this type of communication is perfectly acceptable, it leaves out a whole world of the use of the voice during sex, which can bring you both much deeper satisfaction and closeness and more fun during lovemaking.

By expressing what you are feeling in the moment, simply and with no desire for movement or goal attainment, you become seen, known, and grounded together in the same present moment. This is powerfully bonding. When one partner is verbally expressing, it's hard for the other not to be present as well. He or she cannot be absent in a fantasy or thought from the past or future when a lover is expressing in the here and now. And that's the magic. Be here. Now. Together.

Just as it was a revelation to me after many years of sexual experience to discover that I had a really hard time keeping my eyes open, so it was enlightening to realize that I expended quite a bit of energy keeping silent! What was I thinking in my silence? Well, a variety of things, depending on the situation and the partner. At times I was mentally making a grocery list (yes, really), and other times, when I was so sexually turned on that I thought I might utter something embarrassing, I purposefully kept quiet. And lots of things in between. When I clammed up, that 75 percent nonverbal communication was certainly getting messages across to my partner, but at the same time, the part of my brain that forms direct sentences and could have been used to bring me back to the present moment was absent, or it was being used for cross-purposes. I was not "here now." In fact, even in the throes of "great sex," I was alone, in my head, in the past or in the future—even just a moment ahead—rather than experiencing a joyous union where my partner and I were *here, now, together.*

When sex is relaxed, there is no goal, no prize at the end that each partner is trying to attain, either together or individually. In this atmosphere of "going nowhere," communication takes on a new meaning and a new depth. You can use your voice to express honestly, calmly, and naturally what you are feeling *now*, and what is happening in your body and your emotions *now*. Your intention to communicate in this way causes you to tune in to what *is* happening now.

What are you feeling in each area and part of your body? What sensations are occurring? Now. Now. Now. Stay here. Be here. Talk about here. Now. I feel. I am. I like. As you tell your partner what you are feeling in your body and in your emotions, you also tell yourself. As you verbalize the way you are feeling, you zero in more closely on those feelings. They become more real, more vivid. It feels liberating when you own your feelings, whether emotions or bodily sensations, and share with absolute honesty exactly what you are feeling.

You should never feel the need to criticize or instruct your partner. As you relax into sex, your verbal communication will naturally take on a calm and languid tone, and you'll be able to relate the nuances of your desires lovingly. Each time you do, you will move closer to your lover. Subtly and softly your communication will deepen. Each time you utter a verbal communication and each time you hear your partner speak during lovemaking, use it as an opportunity to sink down deeper into the now. Relax your body and mind, and listen. Tune in. Take it slow. You don't have to help your partner attain anything; there is nothing to accomplish, and there is nowhere you need to go.

When you are talking in the present tense to your partner, expressing your actual experience in this moment, you cannot be somewhere else in your mind or focus. As the Jewish Buddha in a joke I've often heard says, "Be here now. Be somewhere else later. Is that so complicated?"

Love in the moment, and love the moment you are in.

I've found that simply pronouncing "I am now here" brings me back when my mind has wandered. Or sometimes when everything feels so wonderful I can hardly believe it, whispering "I am now here" is like an affirmation that, yes, this is what I'm feeling, this is where I am, and this, for as long as we allow it and make this moment last, is where I choose to stay.

You may be surprised when, in total relaxation and ecstasy, you suddenly hear your partner's voice. As you notice, you sink even further into the present, and yet another layer of the here and now is revealed to you. You can find no end of appreciation for what you are now feeling and for what you are now experiencing.

You may feel vulnerable at first, as I did, when trying to verbally express your emotional and physical sensations during lovemaking. Try to gently push yourself through this discomfort. It might be a surprise to you when you find that your partner actually likes to hear what you have to say and especially enjoys hearing you utter what feels good. Your lover's delight in hearing your sounds and words will motivate you to continue being expressive in this way. You just have to start.

As with any new habit, expressing yourself takes practice. At first, all this tuning in to your body may spark thoughts in your mind, like "I feel ...," which can quickly move on to "I wish he or she ...," and very quickly you've moved beyond the actual present moment. When you say out loud rather than just think, "I feel ...," you've grounded that feeling in the now, and you've shared it with your partner, who is now able to move with you, feel with you, and understand your experience more intimately. This frees energy and allows a wonderful flow to move through your lovemaking.

If you feel yourself stopping and thinking that you can only go so far in your verbal communication, or you find yourself thinking or feeling something that your first instinct is to keep hidden, try to relax deeply and focus more intently, and then share your feeling with your partner. When you're hiding something, it becomes energy that is forced into a holding pattern. As you open up with voice, you release that energy and allow a wonderful unfolding. Practice. Each time you use this key, you'll feel more open, free, and energetic.

What about sounds you make that are nonverbal? Most of us are familiar with the famous scene from the 1989 movie *When Harry Met Sally* where the Meg Ryan character shows the Billy Crystal character how women might fake orgasms. She certainly seems convincing as she moans, shouts, and sighs her way to seeming ecstasy. Have you purposely used sounds to give your partner the impression that he or she is doing something right? Keep in mind that this kind of nonverbal sound is not an authentic sexual sound, so what you gain in temporarily achieving some aim with this deception, you lose in terms of authenticity.

When you are completely relaxed, you might make sounds that are not words, and you want to allow that, but when your partner is aware and grounded with you in the here and now, he or she will be sensitive to the authenticity of your sounds. Truly authentic nonverbal sounds are endearing and sweet (no matter their volume or intensity), while inauthentic sounds are confusing and manipulative.

You may be thinking that you already communicate verbally during sex and that you are actually quite uninhibited at doing so. That's great! I would, however, ask you to examine the things you habitually say to see if they are keeping you *here now*, or if they are moving you into the future, toward a goal, a purpose. Are you using your voice to communicate to your partner that the sex act is moving toward "success"? In relaxed sex, with no goal or success to attain, your verbal communication will take on a different flavor.

If you are used to conventional, goal-oriented sex and are accustomed to voice communication while lovemaking, you may want to rein in your words a bit and make sure that everything you utter really is about the present moment and what you are feeling in it, rather than about driving on to orgasmic excitement. For you, it may take practice to speak only about the present, finely-tuned-in moment. Try to speak only of your own sensations, in the focused present. You don't have to communicate what you need to "get you there," since there is no place to go. You've already arrived!

It's fine to ask your lover questions as you make love, but be sure you keep your awareness focused on the now sensations rather than on the goal of orgasm. Ask your partner how something feels, or what might feel better, but always in a calm and focused manner, where both of you are enjoying the long, relaxed, present moment.

You'll see that in bringing your full consciousness to the moment and setting aside any worry of outcome for either one of you, your sensations will become more available to you, more intense and pleasurable, and your verbal communication with your partner will sustain this. Express your joy, express your pleasure, and fine-tune your description of what is happening.

As with any habit, your habitual verbalization may have lost its meaning and become a ritualized part of lovemaking.

Sometimes we fall into habits that, while they may have been exciting at first, have become simple scripts that we've memorized and are not any deep and actual description of what we are feeling and doing in the moment. If this has happened to you, allow yourself to be silent for a bit, then gradually open up and speak your simple truth. You'll feel the difference immediately. Have no thought of how your utterances are affecting your partner, and try to release any thought of your partner's judgment of what you are saying.

Speak truthfully from your authentic core. You'll find you don't need many words, and the ones you choose will flow easily from your heart. Start your sentences with "I." "I feel..." "I like..." "I am..." Every cell in your body will respond to your verbal offering. Your body knows when you are speaking your truth and when you are withholding or manipulating it. When you allow yourself to be vulnerable by saying exactly what you are feeling, your body comes alive and releases itself ever more to the present. You become more alive each time you offer up your truth.

Removing Masks

It's possible that you've been covering up your truth with a kind of mask. In fact, it's likely. We all do it. Even during the most intimate moments of lovemaking, you may have offered your lover only a masked you to an extent. We do this to cover up various discomforts, or we may don a mask to temporarily be "someone else"—a less inhibited someone perhaps, or someone less vulnerable.

These masks may become so familiar and habitual that we are not aware of putting them on as we come to the sex act. A friend once said to me that when she finally realized she had been putting on masks, she realized she had one for her workplace, one for shopping, one for dealing with her children's teachers, and one for sex! My friend is not a dishonest person. She, like all of us, used the masks to fortify herself with the attributes she wanted to own when doing each of these activities. A much better way to attain these attributes for real, however, is to remove the mask and own the way our unmasked self is feeling. When you make an effort to remove the masks, you may be pleasantly surprised to find that nothing was missing after all.

Your lover doesn't want to make love with the mask nearly as much as he or she wants to make love with the authentic and vulnerable, real you. By the same token, your lover wants his or her own authentic self to be welcomed and adored. In relaxed sex, this can happen naturally and lovingly. Each time you speak out loud from your authentic core, part of your mask will fall away. This will feel like such a relief! Though you may not be consciously aware of wearing the mask, and though speaking your truth through it may be uncomfortable at first, the final result will always be liberating and feel wonderful.

We block true intimacy by not allowing our partners to know exactly what we are feeling. Usually this is for fear of judgment. Remember, you can't experience a lack of judgment until you open up and allow your partner in. It takes a leap of faith at first, but when you've stood (or lain) unmasked with your partner and experienced true acceptance, you will agree that the perceived risk was so very worth taking.

Remember, the key of verbal communication is asking you to try something new. Before you utter a word, ask yourself how authentic and present-based what you are about to say is. Move just a tiny bit past your comfort zone. If you are accustomed to saying nothing at all during lovemaking, start by simply uttering your lover's name. Say simply "yes." Whisper. Hum. Sing. A little discomfort is natural as you try a new behavior. Each time you do, the mask will crumble a little more.

As speaking your feelings in the present moment becomes an easier and more natural habit, you'll find your own power, and it will become clear to you that you hold the keys to your own fulfillment and joy within yourself. Your partner is not responsible for your experience; you are in charge. You have the ability to mold every sexual encounter into something beautiful and satisfying. As you speak your truth, you actually move into closer alignment with your spirit, your inner, non-physical self. In so doing, you make yourself ever more available to your lover. It is a magical unfolding. I don't want you to miss it! Don't worry about sounding "wrong" or "off." Try to speak, each time a little more. Or if you've always been a talker during sex, try to refocus your speech, putting emphasis on simple truths in the present moment.

So do you have to chirp like a chatterbox the whole time you are making love? Of course not. At times no words will come, or you will be so immersed in the beauty of the moment that a voice would pierce uncomfortably into your world. Honor those moments, and be silent when it feels right. Keep relaxing. As you relax, the key of voice communication will begin to feel easier, and you'll know exactly when to use it and when not to. Experiment with talking a little or a lot. Use this key as you do with the others—when needed or intuitively desired.

Peter:

Most anyone who knows us will tell you that Jody and I are master communicators. World-class talkers, if you will. We both make our livings with recorded and written words, and neither of us is the tongue-tied type in any way.

Jody and I have traveled together for months and months on road trips, and it's not unusual for us to drive for hours on end never once turning on the car radio or popping in a CD or MP3. Instead, we chat endlessly about life, love, metaphysics, and a million other things. "Dead air" is a term broadcasters use. Jody and I rarely have any dead air between us. If we are silent, it is while sharing the beauty of the vista that unfolds before us, or simply being quiet in each other's presence, enjoying the moment.

We assumed that all of this talking must mean that we were completely open to one another and that we shared, well, everything! When we began our Tantric sex journey, however, we noticed that in bed, for the most part, silence reigned. There was the usual sigh or moan but rarely any direct verbal communication between us. What did that mean? We wanted to find out, and to take our spiritual lovemaking practice to the next level. Being the great talkers that we are, we undertook the practical research on the key of voice communication with an easy confidence. Surely we would have no trouble being as chatty during sex as we were at other times.

It became apparent, however, that speaking out loud while locked in a sexual embrace was far different than having a regular conversation. At first, it felt a long way from natural. Yes, there was squirming involved. We were aware that our purpose was to stay grounded in the present moment, and we resolved to talk about what was happening at that moment in our bodies. We found that speaking to each other in this way required some focus and a great deal of practice for both of us.

I found this key a bit more natural, since all along, if either of us had talked during lovemaking, it would have been me. It comes more naturally for me to speak candidly about what's happening with my body during lovemaking than it does for Jody. I enjoy saying "that feels wonderful" and putting words to my sensations as I go. It also feels freeing for me to make sounds during lovemaking.

My habit was to speak to Jody during lovemaking by asking her questions. My early attempts sometimes fell short. I would say something like, "What do you need?" She later told me this sounded as if I were asking her what I should do next to keep her on the track to orgasm—not exactly a relaxed approach. So I switched to "Does this feel good?" This sometimes had the desired effect (opened her up to describing her feelings), and other times she simply ignored me, which was okay too. We progressed when I learned to prompt Jody a little bit by asking her to "report in." I would ask her what she was feeling *right now*. In time, we learned to just relax and allow the words to come of their own accord.

Our biggest breakthrough came after months of spiritual lovemaking and appreciation for the concept of relaxation. I began, at moments of quiet during sex, to have the impulse to simply say, "Relax." Now, when I say this word, I mean it as a reminder for both of us. It always has a powerful effect. For Jody, hearing that simple suggestion to relax will cause her to check back in with her body and release any tension. Almost always, it will also cause her to slow down or even stop all movement. This allows an amping up of the focus, a shift in energy, almost a reset that never fails to lift us to new heights of sensation. It has the same effect on me, even when I am the one uttering the word. We immediately become body conscious and do a status check of all our systems, so to speak. "Relax" has become a sort of code word for "Be here now...focus...stay with me here...slow down."

It is easy to retreat into your own little world while making love. You can be physically present and at the same time not really there. Only when Jody and I began intentionally speaking to each other in the right now did we realize how often we had kept those masks on in the past. Even two people as open and verbal as we are found that these attempts to talk while having sex (some more successful than others) served to keep us grounded in the moment and accentuate our enjoyment.

What is really important to remember is that it's not about telling your partner what to do next or giving any kind of instructions. It's talking about what you're feeling right at this instant. Rather than a commentary, it's more of a reporting. There is no judgment.

Voice communication takes you right down to where the rubber meets the road. Just as with eye contact, it's easy to lose focus and drift off course, but by gently reminding each other to stay in the present and stay stripped-down and authentic, real communication can happen, and the bond between you will strengthen even further.

An Exercise in Verbal Communication

When you first read this exercise, you may be tempted, as we were, to assume it's elementary and too easy. Don't be deceived. Make time to try it and give it a serious go. You'll be surprised at its power.

Lie down on a bed, naked, with your partner. If the room is chilly, cover up with a sheet or blanket, but keep your bodies several inches apart, with no physical contact. Look at your lover's eyes, or close your eyes, but do not reach out. Simply tune in carefully to the sensations of your own body. You will feel your partner's energy and proximity, and your own various sensations, but there is no activity to distract you from simply tuning in to how you feel.

After a few minutes of quietly tuning in, start to speak, each in turn. The woman can say what she is feeling in her body first. It might be something like, "I feel a pulse in my temples" or "I feel goosebumps rising on my arms." Or it might be "I feel silly and a little embarrassed." Then let the man express his feelings. Hold back nothing that comes to mind in the description of your physical or emotional feelings. Remember, you're talking about how you feel, not about what you are thinking. There is a subtle difference, and our feelings do arise from our thoughts, but try to start each sentence with "I feel…"

This exercise is not meant to be a conversation. As your partner expresses what he or she is feeling, just listen and accept. Don't offer a response or ask any questions. If your partner says, "I am afraid…," don't offer any analysis or discussion of the feeling. Stay in the present. Hear and accept. Keep your sentences simple and very specific, and try not to allow long pauses or silences. Just keep saying, "I feel…"

Beginning with "I feel" will remind you each time you utter something that you are in the present tense. You are reporting your right-now feeling rather than a want, a desire, a hope, or something in the past.

Sincerity is of the utmost importance. Don't report what you wish you were feeling, but rather report what you *do* feel. You may surprise yourself. After all, this verbal communication can open you up as much to your own feelings as to your partner's. There may even be tears or eruptions of emotion that feel out of place. Allow them. Let them have their expression, and keep reporting your feelings as each new moment presents itself.

Do not try to pretend something is happening if it is not. You might want to say, "I feel so happy lying quietly close to you." If this is your feeling, report it. However, never say something because you want to elicit a particular reaction from your partner. Stick with "just the facts," with no purpose or agenda.

It may help to set a timer. Start with just a few minutes the first time you attempt this exercise. Each time, as you become more comfortable with this, add more time. You will be pleasantly surprised to find that with only a few attempts, you will become better at this and will even look forward to the exercise. When the exercise ends, you may naturally embrace and lovemaking may ensue, or you may simply fall asleep or get up and go about your day. Whatever happens, the energy exchange you have just put into play, enhanced and magnified by the verbal exchange, will stay with you, and nourish you and your relationship.

KEY SIX

Genital Consciousness

Energy follows imagination.
—Diana Richardson

You've probably read the title of this chapter several times and scratched your head wondering, "Does this mean my genitals have consciousness? Or is it about me being conscious *of* my genitals?" The answer to both questions is yes!

Bear with me and I think you'll be a little surprised, as I was, to find out your body, and especially your genitals, have what Diana Richardson calls "intelligence." Yes, you might even say they think for themselves. No, I'm not talking about a man thinking with his penis in the way we usually joke about this. I mean that the male and female genitals feel and generate out of their own innate knowledge of the sex act. I'm talking about *really* tuning in and being deeply aware of the messages your generative organs are sending and receiving. You'll be surprised that when you become truly conscious of your genitals and they are allowed to *be* conscious, they won't be urging you to "get to orgasm quick!" Rather, you'll discover a whole world of sensation that neither you nor your genitals could be aware of until you begin to ... relax into sex.

So what does it mean to have genital consciousness? Starting with being conscious of your genitals, it simply means *feel* them. Really feel them. Put your focus on your penis or your vagina, vaginal area, and clitoris. Purposefully maintain focus on your genitals. Pull your awareness into them. Now, you are probably thinking that this sounds a lot like traditional sex. After all, we're used to focusing on the genitals and their sensations, purposely trying to make them feel more excitement and driving them to orgasm. However, relaxed sex is asking for a different kind of focus. You will feel *more*—but not more excitement and urgency. You will feel more sensitivity, more openness, more connectedness.

Notice I said focus on *your* penis or vagina. We're not talking about trying to figure out what your partner is feeling, and this isn't about trying to excite your partner's genitals or hoping your partner will excite yours. Genital consciousness is about focusing into and feeling your own genitals. It's about allowing them to awaken to their own consciousness, slowly, freely.

When you place your focused awareness on your own penis or vagina while relaxing, you'll discover that they are capable of a large spectrum of sensations you probably had not experienced previously because you were tense and goal oriented. This was my experience, and it was a revelation! I didn't think I could really feel the inside of my vagina, and I certainly had never relaxed for hours during lovemaking, allowing relaxed sex to show its finer sensations to me. Doing this made me feel like I was being introduced to my body for the very first time. Release from the goal and tension of traditional sex opened up the possibility of feeling *all* of what my body was capable of.

The first thing to do when trying to be conscious of your genitals and allowing them to be conscious is to *slow down*.

In fact, if you are like me, in order to slow down and release tension, you truly need to stop all action for a time. Allow yourself to be at complete rest. Don't be afraid to lie still for what may seem like a long period of time. Lie still in consciousness and just feel. When you feel totally relaxed, relax even more, focusing on letting go, and then letting go a little more.

Men sometimes have been advised to slow down their lovemaking to allow their partner to catch up or not be left behind. This makes sense, however, only if a race toward orgasm is going on. It implies a goal, an ending, a place you are both trying to reach. This is not the case in relaxed sex! Relaxed sex and the key of genital consciousness ask you to slow down, not just to prolong lovemaking but to enhance it and to experience it more fully. Don't be afraid to slow down. Don't be afraid to periodically cease all movement. Relax.

This key is not so much about concentrating (which takes effort) on the genitals as it is about allowing them to do what they already know how to do, and allowing them to feel what they already know how to feel. It's about tuning in and asking them what they feel, rather than doing things *to* the genitals in an attempt to make them feel. Bring your focus to your genitals in a softly open and questioning manner.

We are accustomed to using friction to bring more sensation to the genitals. Most of us are not aware, however, that friction actually makes the organs less sensitive over time. During conventional lovemaking, the man will often be focused only on the sensitive tip of his penis, and the woman on the sensations in her clitoris. The rest of the genitalia are called into play for purposes of the friction that we've been taught will excite these sensitive areas. As each partner moves, thrusting the pelvis, the friction accomplishes its purpose of creating sexual excitement for both partners, and the shaft of the penis and the inner folds of the vagina are mostly desensitized. Our consciousness may be focused on sexual sensation, but it is not focused on the entirety of the genitals. In this type of conventional lovemaking, we lose the infinite nuances of sensation that are available when we slow down, focus, and allow genital consciousness its power.

Penetration

The moment of initial penetration of penis into vagina can be slowed down considerably. Penetration creates the environment and sets the tone for the lovemaking session, so for relaxed sex, slow down penetration. Allow the penis to enter the vagina in tiny increments. Each time it probes a bit deeper, stop. Be conscious of the entire organ. Be aware. The penis and vagina will communicate naturally with one another and with you. Allow this to occur, and delight in the new sensations. You have no place to go and nothing to accomplish. Only this moment of deep communion, sensitivity, and connection exists. Relax. Allow.

The genitals know what to do. Remember, they have *intelligence*, and without the customary friction, they will wake up and take on a life of their own. Allow the penis to stop, relax, and enjoy the vaginal environment in an unhurried way. Notice every nuance of sensation, and rejoice in the completeness of the experience of being connected this way, needing to go nowhere and accomplish nothing.

Relaxing the Vagina

Most women, as they become sexually excited through friction, will tense up the vaginal muscles. Often a woman will deliberately tighten these muscles at the outset of penetration because she believes (erroneously) that the man needs a tight and tense vaginal environment for his own sensations to be satisfying. Some women are concerned that childbearing or aging may have caused the vagina to become too loose. This fear can trigger a deliberate or unconscious tensing of the vagina and pelvic area. If you are one of these women, you'll be interested to know that actually this tension does not increase the sensitivity of the penis during lovemaking but in fact does just the opposite!

When you relax into sex, as the vagina and penis are allowed to simply *be* rather than *do*, their natural *intelligent* sensations will arise and you'll experience even greater sexual ecstasy than before, when friction and tension were employed. So no matter what condition you believe your vagina is in, you can allow it to access its own *intelligence*. Try not to bring tension of any kind to the area. This might take practice, but it's worth it. Every bit of tension you release will allow you to dip into deeper relaxation and ultimately even more intense sensation, for you and for your lover.

When the two of you try being connected with no movement for the first time, penis in vagina, you may be a bit dismayed at how little you actually feel. Don't be discouraged. Allow for a time of simply being quiet and relaxed and waiting for the sensations to occur. They will. Meanwhile, you can keep asking your body, and especially your genital area, to relax even more deeply. The energy will flow back and forth and in a circular path through and between your bodies as you stop *doing* and start *being*.

Peter:

I think most men will agree that we usually "speak" to our penis in rather direct, simple messages. We direct our sexual instrument from the prelude to the crescendo. Over and over again, we bring ourselves—and hopefully our partner—to a wonderful finish. Ta da! Great performance! We take a bow and exit. There is very little tuning in to the instrument on our part in this scenario we've practiced since our earliest sexual experience.

As with the other keys to spiritual lovemaking, I resolved to see what this one was all about. I decided to be an observer, zeroing in on my own penis as an attentive watcher and listener. As I practiced that, I became conscious of my genitals in a whole new way. I discovered that there really was a wonderful, rejuvenating energy pulsing beneath the surface of full-friction sex, and it was communicating to me. At first, it was like trying to hear a whispered conversation in the middle of a crowded party. What was required of me was to wait quietly, tune out the noise, and let the party disperse.

So how do you tune out the "noise"?

To learn how to focus consciousness on the genitals for an extended period of time, I found my meditation practice to be a big help. You don't need to have an established meditation practice to understand genital consciousness, but what I'm going to share with you here is a close cousin to meditation of other kinds. The only real thing that you are tasked with in meditation is to continually bring your focus back to your breathing, thereby releasing thought. Here, you are doing much the same thing, but instead of focusing on your breath, you bring your attention to your own genitals. I'm talking about the genital area in its entirety. As a man, I would most often focus on the "business end" of my penis. Once I learned to consider what was going on there as that "noisy party" I mentioned, I discovered that if I let things quiet down, I began to really feel the shaft, the base, and all around that most wonderfully sensitive region.

We are used to being in the driver's seat of sex, so to speak. The key of genital consciousness gives you the chance to become a passenger, leaning back against the tuck-and-roll upholstery and feeling the wind in your hair while admiring the sky, knowing that the perfect driver is at the wheel. Now *that* is a spiritual experience!

As Jody often reminds me, the body knows what to do. Your genitals know intrinsically what they are doing, and if you can stop running the show for a while, you will be surprised at the energies and pleasures you and your partner's genitals know how to generate on their own.

An Exercise in Genital Consciousness

Sit with your partner in a yab-yum position (the man sits with his legs crossed in "Indian" or "Lotus" style, while the woman, facing him, sits on his lap with her legs straddling his body). Make yourselves comfortable with pillows on the floor or against the wall or backboard of the bed. Ensure that you will both be completely at ease for a while. You can insert penis into vagina, or simply gently touch them to one another. It's okay to close your eyes here if it helps you focus your mind on your own genital area.

Now gently bring your focus to your breathing. As your mind quiets, bring your attention down to your genitals. Try to tune in to what they are feeling. Drift in and out of this focus if it feels hard to maintain. If you feel your attention drifting, simply shift yourself or move slightly. Feel the warmth and weight of your partner's body, and be conscious briefly of that connection. Then return to your genitals. Silently ask them to communicate with you. Continue to meditate in this way, with your attention on your genitals. You may have the urge to move. Follow this impulse. Almost imperceptibly slow and easy movements are the way to go.

It may take some time for true sensitivity to return to your genitals. It reminds me of heading home after a rock concert when I was a kid. Sometimes the ringing in my ears went on for hours, and I certainly wouldn't have heard anything as subtle as a rustling of leaves along the way—at least not until after a morning recovery. Your genitals have been speaking in boisterous voices for a while now, so be prepared for "the gap."

The first few times you try this, you may feel almost completely numb to any subtleties down there. Be patient with yourself and with your genitals. After all, you and they are used to movement bringing sensation, so being still and quiet may feel like…nothing. Tell yourself that you may be doing "nothing," but you are not feeling "nothing." Allow the feelings to arise from the depths. When you begin by doing "nothing," you are relinquishing control and letting your genitals take over. They will tell you to move and shift and reposition yourself in smooth and subtle ways. We will talk about this more in the key of rotating positions.

Rest assured that after some practice at genital consciousness, the penis and vagina will begin to lead the way. Then the magic will begin.

KEY SEVEN

Soft Penetration

Traditional sex is a series of collisions.
Relaxed sex is more of a blending.
—Peter Beamish

At the beginning of the book, I mentioned that most of us know the how-tos of sex, as in what goes where and what has to move to create the friction that creates excitement and leads to orgasm. And when we've talked about penetration, it's been assumed, most likely, that it's the erect penis that is penetrating the vagina. A fair assumption. That is usually true. And, well, if you are like me, the idea of soft penetration will be surprising and perplexing at first, but you'll soon find it delightful and enlightening.

No Erection Required

I confess that my first reactions to the concept of making love when the penis is not "ready" were disbelief and laughter. It seemed a little ridiculous! It didn't take much convincing, however, for me to begin to understand. I decided this idea might have some merit after giving some serious thought to the overall concept of relaxed sex. After all, I reasoned, the man is certainly more relaxed when his penis is relaxed, and vice versa. This new idea, which may seem counterintuitive at first, can end up being amazingly rewarding.

I know this is a bit of a delicate subject. Many men feel embarrassed or inadequate when the penis doesn't attain or maintain an erection in response to stimulation. And women who don't understand fully the way the erectile response works may erroneously believe it is their lover's lack of physical attraction for them that is causing what is perceived as a problem. Men sometimes even apologize, as if they've committed a sexual faux pas by being near their lover with the intention to make love and then not having the proper, um, tools to make it happen.

Men reading this may nod in knowing agreement when I say that a soft penis most certainly does not indicate a lack of attraction or desire! Women, please take heart and understand that this is true. While it's beyond the scope of this book to discuss what could be causing a lack of erection in any given man, in any given situation, it is important that we understand here that it does not have to mean you can't make love, and it does not have to mean either partner can't feel as much joy and satisfaction (yes, even physical satisfaction) from making love using soft penetration.

The penis in its non-erect state is capable of penetrating the vagina.

This is a new idea for you, no doubt. So, I'll repeat: The penis in its non-erect state (for whatever reason it may find itself in such a state) *is* capable of penetrating the vagina.

For you and your lover, the soft-state penis may be a rare occurrence, as it was for me and Peter as we explored the Tantric principles, or it might be more often the case than not. Whichever is true for you, I can promise that adding soft penetration to your toolbox of ideas and possibilities will enhance your understanding and practice of relaxed sex.

The penis and vagina are amazing and powerful instruments of energy transfer, but when we cause them to be numb in their very excitement (as can happen during friction sex), they lose some of their ability to connect energetically. By using soft penetration, we give them a chance to reconnect and regain their energetic integrity. Through soft penetration, we discover the result of relaxed sensation leading to the natural polarity between the partners being engaged. Ahhhh... heightened relaxation, heightened sensation.

Men may raise an eyebrow at first but will eventually embrace this key as a revelation and a welcome surprise. *"You mean I don't always have to be hard?"* This can be a relief, and liberating in its simple truth. The decision to experiment with soft penetration releases the man from performance anxiety. Oh, and size *really* does not matter.

When a couple agrees to try soft penetration, they will come together naturally in a much less tension-filled state. Sexual excitement will happen, but first a deep connection, a relaxed energetic state, and a true communication between penis and vagina will take place. Soft penetration allows both partners to warm up simultaneously, and usually the rise of desire, if it happens, will be equal as the genitals communicate without tension or friction.

Tips and Techniques for Soft Penetration

Okay, let's say you're sold and want to try soft penetration. How is it done? Like me, you have probably assumed that if the penis isn't erect, it doesn't really belong in the vagina. Yet soft penetration is actually an easy skill to learn, and after the first time, you might even say, "Why didn't I think of that?"

So here's how to do it. Any position might work, but we have found that the easiest is the missionary position, with man on top. The woman or the man can take the penis between two fingers, gently stretch toward the opening of the vagina, and insert it.

Another good position for soft penetration is when the man lies on his side facing the woman. The woman lies on her back, bringing her pelvis close to his. Both open their legs and the genitals will be lying opposite each other. Bring them together and wrap your legs around each other. This is sometimes called the scissors position. The woman may have to move her upper body away from her lover's in order to make the pelvises fit, or she can angle her own pelvis upward.

Be gentle and take your time. It's really not difficult. Use the suggestions here or find your own position by experimenting. Using a lubricant sometimes can help. Our favorite is virgin coconut oil. The beauty of soft penetration is that since both partners are fairly relaxed and not in a frenzied state of sexual excitement, they can gently insert the penis in whatever way seems most natural and comfortable.

The woman must keep her vagina relaxed when her partner is attempting soft penetration because nothing is pushing its way past the vaginal entrance. Instead, the penis is being welcomed in, and this must be through a completely open door. By opening her mouth slightly and relaxing her lips, the woman sends an energetic message to the vaginal opening to yield. She might also exhale softly, keeping the lips of the mouth relaxed, and visualize the vaginal lips and walls parting. Relax. Opening is natural.

Once the soft penis is inside, stop all movement for a time, and just let go. Allow the natural energies of the genitals to mingle and communicate. This can be a time of profoundly deep closeness between you and your lover. When the woman tells her partner that she feels the energy of his penis even though it is not erect, this can come as a relief and a pleasant surprise to him. So communicate and relax. Relax and communicate. Use the rest of the keys as you focus your mind and body on the present moment. When you are connected in this manner and truly allowing of whatever might follow, you will begin to feel the penis come alive and give forth energetic signals.

When the man consciously relaxes while he is soft inside the vagina, his penis may gradually become erect as if drawn up into the depths of the vagina with an intelligence of its own. The penis will usually become erect at some point while inside the vagina; it may grow, then soften, and then enlarge again in its own rhythm. Allow the natural polarity of your bodies to take over, and watch and feel with fascination the dance that occurs when everything is relaxed. Take note of the nuances of sensation you may never have felt before.

Don't worry if you don't feel much of anything the first time you try soft penetration. Remember that you've probably trained the penis to expect friction to feel sexual sensation, and it may take some time for it to relax into its natural ability to channel energy without action or erection. The vagina, too, has become accustomed to friction, and often we are not aware of how much sensation it is capable of until we stop, connect softly, and wait. Just lie quietly and allow your bodies to radiate energy in natural polarity.

If you have time, it's actually possible and very wonderful to lie together connected in this way for hours, feeling a depth of connection and genital communication beyond what was possible before. It is so very much worth the effort to feel the special sensations that are possible when you make love without effort or strain.

Go ahead and give it a try. Just plug in, and see what happens. Connect your bodies just for the sake of connection and not to move them to completion of anything. For what can turn out to be a profound change, *start* with penetration. The concept of foreplay doesn't have meaning here because you are not using penetration *before* anything! You are just being here now, with no beginning and no ending to the experience other than what you choose. No event need happen. Just being close. Breathing. Perhaps talking together, bodies connected. Your sexual energy will be activated in these moments, but not necessarily your sexual excitement.

Soft penetration is one of those things in relaxed sex that is not intuitive for those of us reared in the second half of the twentieth century, so I'm asking you to try it not once but several times before you judge its value. Really and truly allowing yourselves to relax into a non-goal-oriented sexual encounter can be so profound that I think you'll be writing to me not long after you read this book to tell me how amazed you are!

Peter:

Ever since adolescence, and into my early years of sexual experience, I always thought it was a given that the man's role and "obligation" in sex included staying completely hard and erect from first attraction throughout a sexual intercourse session until orgasm. Anything less than a very firm penis would be showing my partner that I was less than enthused or not turned on.

I thought you had to be erect right at the outset, even as you were taking off your clothes, because being excited meant being immediately hard. Everything in our society points toward big, hard, and long-lasting, and the idea that a soft, flaccid penis could be anything other than a liability, or a "time out" from sex, just doesn't compute for most men. I am here to tell you that making love with a soft penis works, and it is the man who will benefit most from this knowledge. Yes, engineering things so that you can go inside a woman while soft requires some concentration and technique, but once you are resting comfortably inside, an entirely new energetic level of give-and-take surfaces.

Be with each other. Enjoy each other. Feel the energy flow between each other, with absolutely no obligation to prove anything to anyone. Freed of any and all requirements to be hard, to move in a certain way, to manage the lovemaking session, or even to please your lover, you can rest naturally in the experience. It's like being on vacation. You don't go on vacation to "get things done." You go simply for the pleasure of it.

I realize now that I had always felt that, as the man, I was the one responsible for everything that happened during lovemaking. And in order to make things happen, I needed (pardon the expression) the right tool. Learning that the erect member is *not* the main thing I bring to a sexual encounter was truly liberating knowledge for me.

As I practiced relaxed sex over time, the notion that a complete erection is always vital slowly gave way to a clear understanding that the penis is "useful" no matter what its state. When I really let go of the idea that I must be "reporting for duty" at all times, it was a game-changer for me.

Further, the discovery that I could participate in really great lovemaking—*even with a soft penis*—was simply astounding. Because remember, we've changed what we define as great lovemaking when we're talking about complete spiritual alignment during sex.

Talk about being able to relax! Men, there is no need to start out with a stiff salute as if reporting for duty. It's great when it happens—which may be most of the time for many of us. But with the pressure removed, a man can truly relax into sex.

When Jody and I first decided to experiment with soft penetration, we both were skeptical. But as earnest sexual explorers, we decided to give it an honest try. I've always felt that great lovemaking sessions include a sprinkling of laughter here and there, and there certainly were some shared giggles as we worked out the engineering behind inserting the soft penis into the vagina. Laughter is good for the soul's alignment and can only improve the experience, so don't be discouraged at the initial awkwardness of the whole thing, and be patient with yourself and your partner as you traverse this new ground.

For me, it works best if I let Jody do the initial manipulation with her own positioning, with her legs and with her hands, to comfortably get me inside. Hand over the remote! Then, once inside, use the rest of your body to make love and let the penis lie back and just be. I find that there is a natural ebb and flow to my hardness, and it has nothing to do with motion. It has to do with where my head is at. As our lovemaking intensifies, I may realize that I am hard again. As we rest and "valley out," my penis relaxes and deflates. And yet there is always a warm energy flow pulsing back and forth between us throughout.

The amazing thing to me is that after we settle in, we literally begin to feel an energetic push and pull—a back and forth, a give-and-take energy exchange, similar to friction sex but on a much subtler level. Again, at first it was like listening to a whispered conversation in a room so loud you could barely hear yourself. Once softly inside the vagina, slow your motion, or just be motionless. Do some gentle meditative breathing, employ the key of genital consciousness as well as the other keys, and let things unfold without any effort on your part.

If you've achieved initial penetration with an erection, it is still possible to move into a soft experience. Relax and allow the penis to go soft again. When I do this, it gives me a wonderful sense of peace, contentment, well-being, and balance. As your penis softens inside your partner, it feels as if you are dissolving into each other. It is as if the boundaries between you are beginning to melt—a very blissful feeling indeed. Simply be present.

Yes, it surprised me, but it was with this key that our lovemaking became truly transformational.

KEY EIGHT

Deep Penetration

Every desire of your body is holy.
—*Hafiz*

As you've read this book, you've likely noticed that the man is often asked to avoid motion that will cause friction and is told that "going for the goal" and trying to achieve orgasm is not what relaxed sex is all about. We've told the man that he can achieve an orgasmic state even if he never actually ejaculates during a lovemaking session. Well, what about the woman? Is she capable of this orgasmic state and the depths of ecstasy without release?

As you've probably guessed, the answer is *yes*.

And, of course, it entails—what else—relaxation and presence. Let go. Be here now. Allowing time, ease, and deep, sustained penetration is one avenue to the "sexual healing" that is possible when partners go the extra millimeter, so to speak.

There is nothing wrong with an orgasm based in the clitoris, and excitement and release there is what most women are accustomed to. Deep penetration offers a different way of reaching the depth and breadth of the female sexual experience.

An Opportunity to Heal

When a woman has experienced any kind of sexual trauma or a negative experience with respect to anything sexual or her physical body, memories of those events can be stored deep within the vaginal and cervical tissue. This cellular memory is evoked when the penis enters the vagina and makes its way into its depths. When the cells reawaken to these feelings, they have an opportunity to heal. We usually do not provide the calm or the relaxation to allow this healing, as we push on with friction. The opportunity, however, can be seized, and we can allow deep penetration to facilitate a feeling of profound and permanent release. By allowing the erect penis to deeply and fully penetrate the vagina slowly and deliberately, polarity is restored, and the power of this healing opportunity is unleashed.

As opposed to the previous key, a full erection is obviously called for here. Yet deep penetration may naturally occur as an outcome of soft penetration. If the penis has entered the vagina while in a relaxed, soft state, and with time has reached its fully erect state, deep penetration will occur as a result, and this is wonderful. It's also possible, of course, for the erect penis to penetrate at the outset. In this case, begin very slowly, with complete conscious awareness. Pause frequently along the way, and focus.

Using the other spiritual lovemaking tools will add greatly to your enjoyment of deep penetration, so make some eye contact, communicate, and breathe deeply as you keep your awareness focused on your genitals. Slowly allow the penis to penetrate until it touches the uppermost end of the vagina. When it arrives at the cervix, bring it back just a tiny bit so there is the slightest bit of space between the end of the vaginal canal and the head of the penis. Then stop. The man can shift his penis gently and slowly from side to side (a technique that can be extremely pleasurable for both partners) but without thrusting or rhythmic pumping.

Just penetrate. Deeply and fully. Then relax. Then wait.

Remember, the actual length of the penis is not important, and even if it does not reach the cervix, if it is completely enveloped in the vagina, the vagina will naturally fold itself around it. I think it bears repeating that size doesn't matter. Deep penetration is actually full penetration. You'll know when you've achieved it.

Allow the genitals to decide what to do next. Bring your awareness and presence fully to the activity of penetrating deeply and being deeply penetrated. Relax the muscles of your extremities.

You may feel a burst of electric ecstasy or a calm glow or even waves of orgasm. Imagine energy being exchanged between, and generated by, the penis and vagina.

After a time of very little physical movement, the man may begin to feel his erection recede or even begin to withdraw slightly. Allow a cycle of natural ebb and flow by remaining still and conscious. Some movement might be called for to attain or sustain erection, but you don't have to attempt to coax the penis back to hard erection by using too much friction or excitement. Allow it to naturally come to fullness again as it experiences the energy of the depths of the vagina.

What if the woman experiences pain during deep penetration? Pain, according to Diana Richardson, can be an indication of cellular memory being activated. Try to slow down and allow any messages to surface. I found it very helpful to realize that when we try to dull physical pain, or to avoid it, we are actually missing an important healing opportunity. If you can, try to be with the pain, and allow it, staying focused on the deep penetration, and asking your body and spirit to release anything it might be holding on to that is not serving you. Of course I am *not* talking here about sharp or excruciating pain, and I would never advise you to neglect any actual physical condition that can and should be remedied in conjunction with this spiritual experience. On the other hand, pain doesn't always indicate that we need an outside practitioner to heal us. I think you'll be quite pleasantly surprised to find that deep sexual penetration, along with profound relaxation, can have an amazingly positive effect and can even cause longstanding discomfort to disappear.

Ever since my first sexual experiences, I remember being uncomfortable when the head of my partner's penis would bump my cervix. Sometimes the pain would even radiate up to my lower abdomen, making me jump and say "ouch!" I assumed this simply meant that the cervix was sensitive and shouldn't be touched, or if touched, only gently. However, I now believe that I was carrying some beliefs, some emotional "baggage" surrounding sex, and some cellular memory of those first painful moments of lovemaking as a young woman. After several sessions of deep penetration as I'm describing it here, the pain began to lose its hold, and

I can now entertain even the deepest thrusting, my cervix feeling resilient and allowing.

The man should not push through the pain. The woman should clearly communicate what she is feeling, while at the same time being open to allowing the pain to communicate and be released. The man can move back very slightly and wait for the pain to subside before gently trying to penetrate deeply again. Allow any emotions that surface to make their presence fully known. Feel them, and express an intention to release them, either silently or with words. If you can stay with it, a new relaxation and vitality will begin to take the place of the pain. Both partners may experience a release of emotions. There might be tears, laughter, relief, and, of course, joy.

Forging a Profound Connection

By using deep, slow, relaxed penetration, we allow polarity to take its natural course. Healing can occur, and a deep, abiding connection is forged between the partners. When you share deep, prolonged penetration, a profound connective experience ensues. You will emerge after a session of deep penetration with a new feeling of closeness to your partner and to your inner being. Remember, allow enough time in a relaxed, calm environment.

Women, you may think you've been penetrated deeply before and it was nothing special. When you *relax* into deep penetration, you'll experience the difference.

The first time Peter and I decided to consciously practice deep penetration and see what we could discover, I became sleepy and almost weary after the penetration itself. I felt my body wanting to simply give way to slumber, and I knew I could stay that way without moving for a very long time. Just as I was thinking these thoughts, Peter said, "I wonder if I could fall asleep like this!" It wasn't just mental telepathy between us; it was the profoundly comfortable and comforting feeling of penetrating and being penetrated and then simply stopping and being. We both felt it as a deep rest, a safety, and a haven. Sleep seemed the next logical step.

I found it humorous that several times when we consciously put deep penetration into practice, Peter did fall asleep for a few minutes, and when he awoke, he was unaware that he'd slipped into slumber. When I told him, he was happy to hear that he'd managed to feel so much relaxation. Once we had the hang of this key, Peter would decide when to employ it, giving me a gentle nudge into deeper relaxation as I surrendered to it and let go of any need to do anything but experience it.

Peter:

When a man has penetrated deeply into his partner with a full erection, it's easy to see why a woman could naturally tend to put up a subtle energetic defense while in such a vulnerable position. There is always the possibility of sudden, abrupt movement that could cause her to instinctively tense and contract. Your lover has probably come to expect the thrusting movements that an erect penis usually seeks, and it can be very helpful to declare your intention to initiate a session of deep penetration. This doesn't mean that she doesn't find the thrusting of an erect penis inside her enjoyable. It means that for the key of deep penetration to be used optimally, she should be able to let go of any tension and any expectation of having to meet a force with a force, so to speak. I find it very helpful to tell Jody, when I've penetrated deeply, "Relax. I'm not going to make any sudden moves." Once she has this reassurance from me, we can both sink even more deeply together into relaxation.

There is nothing like being enveloped inside a woman while being vibrantly hard, and although a man's natural instinct is toward a continuous in-and-out motion, by choosing to remain almost motionless—parked, as it were—and by being a little bit patient, you will start a subtle yet very strong sexual energy flow between you and your partner. There really *is* a magnetic attraction that can be felt by the head of your penis, but most men never experience this due to the friction and frenzy of their movements.

I find that the traditional in-and-out motion can be replaced by a gentle side-to-side rocking at times, and it has a very soothing effect on us both. This new "love language" is very subtle, and all I can tell you is that when listened to, it results in feelings and sensations that are deeper and richer than those experienced by friction sex.

KEY NINE

Positions

Move and the way will open.
—Zen proverb

You might be thinking, "Oh great, now comes the part where we are told to put tab A into slot B." Let me assure you that this key is nothing at all like the instructions for putting together your child's last Christmas present. Nor is relaxing into sex like a sport, with maneuvers that have to be learned, coached, and practiced. In fact, nothing could be further from the truth.

Rotating Positions Naturally

When you relax into sex, as I hope you are aware by now, you do just that—relax! So the positions, for the most part, take care of themselves. I'm sure it will come as no surprise when I tell you to just do whatever feels most natural and comfortable. Rotating positions is about maximum connection and genital contact; it's not about trying to contort ourselves to get maximum excitement or friction for any particular body part. Knowing this is so freeing and so, well, relaxing!

The best position for you and your partner will not be exactly the same as for any other couple. The position that allows for the easiest, most natural genital contact is the best for you. You'll ease naturally into your preferred position as you allow polarity and relax into connection with your lover.

Since sexual energy is dynamic and keeps changing and shifting, you will want to do the same with your bodies. Follow any impulse that arises to move and rotate, but avoid creating the kind of rhythmic excitement that leads to release or ejaculation. Allow the ebb and flow of sexual feeling as you remain motionless for a time, followed by a naturally occurring shift in position. You may shift as often as you like, but without urgency and without stress. Your movements will flow together as you become closer and more connected with each rotation.

Start by finding a position where your pelvic areas are firmly in contact with each other. The initial position should allow for both partners to completely relax into a feeling of soft, supportive comfort. Keep the genitals as the focus of your contact, and find the best way for them to connect. Think of coming together in order to *be* together, and don't thrust and grind as in traditional sex. Allow your bodies to connect and then immediately relax. Once you have found this primary position, you can use it to rotate around as often as you like during your lovemaking session.

The penis should be inserted into the vagina. Hold the initial position for a time, and then shift. With your "I am here now" consciousness softly in mind, you will find that you and your partner will move together as one unit of energy. Relax and stay alert to your bodies' signals. Your bodies will tell you when it's time to move slightly or to completely change position. At times you may find yourselves almost too comfortable, and a sleepy or drowsy state may come over you. When you notice this, slowly shift to another position, and tune in yet again with focused genital consciousness.

If you find yourself in a position you haven't tried before, or one that feels unnatural or that makes you feel more vulnerable than you are used to, try to hold that position briefly rather than immediately shifting away toward the more familiar. Give yourself time to energetically and mentally explore this new territory. In relaxed sex, these unfamiliar positions may have something to offer that you had not considered before. Each position will give you a new perspective. As you hold positions without moving, as opposed to what is done in traditional sex, you give yourself a chance to learn what it feels like to be connected in new ways.

Experiment.

Take your time.

You may find that the positions you've been using for quite some time and that you thought were the best for you were actually simply the most sexually exciting or the most familiar and safe. Give yourself a chance to experience the almost infinite number of positions that are available. Each can open up a new vista, as each physical position comes with a new mental and emotional position. As you rotate to different positions, try to relax into each one and take time to just *be*.

Nowhere to go.

Nothing to do.

Just be.

At times during relaxed sex, you may think you should be doing more, and your mind may try to take over and make you more active. The old mindset of having to stimulate your partner or help him or her reach an excited state may try to intervene. Each time this happens, try to relax again, and as you sink into each new position, allow yourself to feel the sensations deeply and enjoy the new perspective.

Peter:

When I mention "Tantric sex" in conversation, it often seems that those who have heard of it have the idea that it mostly entails couples making love for hours and hours on end. Sometimes they'll say, "How is this possible?" And indeed, when thought of in terms of conventional friction sex, sure, in and out for hours on end sounds exhausting—and in the case of male stamina, almost unbelievable.

But with relaxed spiritual sex, I've discovered that once I am plugged-in and comfortably positioned, I really can enjoy myself for hours on end. In fact, with the use of some strategically placed pillows and the nearby availability of a glass of water and some delectable pieces of fruit, it is not only possible, but extremely pleasurable and rewarding. Jody and I can remain connected and relaxed to the point where we can softly stroke each other, chat here and there, and even—to my wondrous surprise—drift in and out of sleep! Gently dozing off while connected at the genitals is a heart-opening experience. Gradually waking again and realizing that I am still "inside" is an almost indescribable pleasure.

Jody and I also have a lot of fun shifting positions, sometimes quite dramatically, while holding tight to one another and rotating as a unit. There can be quiet intensity or lighthearted giggling involved as you and your partner make subtle shifts while keeping your focus on the "seal" between your genitals.

Be imaginative but not acrobatic. Be curious as to the many ways your bodies can connect around the genitals, and stay open to trying something new. If the penis slips out, simply reinsert it and relax back into a comfortable position. Move as a unit. Alternate naturally between taking the lead and following. As one partner feels the need to move and shift, the other follows gently.

As you *relax into sex* more and more deeply, you may surprise yourself by finding that positions you once thought were uncomfortable for you, or that you didn't feel would be a good fit for you, are now perfectly natural and easy. When performing isn't necessary and you have nothing to be good at or to master, rotating positions becomes a joy and happens naturally. Stay open and curious. You and your partner will no doubt develop favorite positions that you'll slip into naturally again and again. These will be conducive to long periods of lovemaking where you relax, close your eyes, and remain connected for perhaps hours at a time.

You will surprise and delight yourself and your partner as you discover new and different *relaxed* positions for love-making.

Epilogue

Relaxed Sex Can Change Your Life

You might find the title to this last part a bit dramatic, and I suppose it is. The thing is, since learning about relaxed sex, my own world has changed, and, well, I would not be telling the truth if I didn't dramatically proclaim my belief that it can, and will, change yours as well, if you let it.

Please make time not just for love, but for lovemaking. It may be fashionable to say that sex isn't important in a relationship, or that intimacy can be achieved without sex, and therefore we need more cuddling or more talking and not as much "plugging in." However, sexual energy is a powerful force, and it is ever present. When we relax, we can uncover treasures we may have been denying by buying into the popular cultural belief that sex is only for the newly in love, the young, or those who have lots of time to spare.

Sex *is* important in a relationship! Don't shortchange yourself or your partner by subscribing to the popular notion that we burn out our need for sex and that it is "overrated." This is simply a response to our misunderstanding of the potential for lovemaking that is not goal oriented, not based on performance, and that is unending in its variety. It is a response to our erroneous thoughts of sex being an activity that depletes our energy rather than a life-giving force that rejuvenates and enlivens us.

Have you seen those polls where couples are asked how often they have sex after one year in their relationship, after ten years, after thirty-five years, and so on? We all look with curiosity to see how we compare in frequency of lovemaking to our peers. Once a week? Twice? None of these polls asks how many hours we spend with our genitals connected to those of our lover. None of them asks how many minutes we look into our partner's eyes. They measure events, not time spent in deep, communal ecstasy. They may as well be asking how many times a week we sneeze or scratch an itch!

Spiritual lovemaking isn't about how many times we perform an activity. It's about relaxing into being all that we can be. It's about being connected to what brings life to life. Yes, lovemaking *is* important to your relationship. So make time, and relax into sex.

Once you've made what I've described in these pages a part of your everyday life, you'll notice a change in every aspect of your consciousness. You'll find yourself seeing your partner, as well as all of the people, places, objects, and situations you encounter, in the light of presence and awareness, and this cannot help but change your perspective dramatically and for the better.

I am now here.

That sentence alone, if you make it your mantra—whether in lovemaking, at work, or in your relationships with family and friends—will shift your energy from past and future awareness to present awareness, and that makes all the difference. It really is true that all we have is the present moment. And living fully within the present moment means just that— living fully.

As Peter said during one of our lighthearted conversations, "Only love heals." Relaxing into sex makes the kind of love we all long for accessible and very, very real. Relax. Be here now. Focus. Feel. Use the keys. Get the video *Relax into Sex* with Big Sur in the background (see the "Recommend Reading and Viewing" section). Relax again. Make love again. Make this an important part of your life. Let us know how your life has changed as a result of experiencing these easy, natural, and old yet new ways of making love.

I've tried to let you know simply and relatively quickly and in my own words how you can *relax into sex*. Now, in the "Recommended Reading and Viewing" section that follows, I'm going to turn you on to some of the material that has been pivotal in my life and in Peter's life. It's often a winding and twisting road as we follow our bliss and our inspiration through piles of books and miles of media. Each of us has our own path as we allow our natural curiosity and inner compass to lead. Having this book in your hands means our paths have somehow converged, so I'm confident that somewhere in the resources section you will find other enlightening and engaging ideas. So enjoy! And relax. It's my intention that this material will joyfully affect your lovemaking and your life.

Jody Baron

2013 and beyond

Recommended Reading and Viewing

The materials listed here have inspired, taught, and positively influenced us. Some have simply entertained us in soft and gentle ways, while others have induced us to make profound, life-changing shifts. Not all these materials are specific to lovemaking, but since all things are interrelated and universal truths are indeed universal, we feel the materials on this list all contribute in one way or another to the understandings and insights that lead to a life of ease, grace, and alignment between our physical and non-physical selves. (They also lead to a life of powerful creation and manifestation!)

The list could be oh so much longer, but we had to limit it somehow, and by starting with any of these materials we think you'll be inspired on your own journey of reading, watching, and listening that will open doors and unveil new vistas for you.

If nothing on this list looks familiar, then you are about to enter a new world of thought. If many or even most of the materials are old hat to you, we suggest exploring something on the list that is new and different, and see where that leads. Let your intuition be your guide, and just jump in.

Baron, Jody, and Peter Beamish. *Relax into Sex: The Art of Spiritual Lovemaking.* DVD. CreateSpace, 2011.

This video takes the information from the book and amps up the relaxing! You'll be making love with your partner to the sound and sight of the waves. Stunning Big Sur visuals and sounds accompany the voices of Leslie Lewis Sword and Peter Beamish, who voice delicious words that will relax you … into lovemaking. You will enjoy the experience of relaxing into sex as this program refreshes the ideas and information from this book and Diana Richardson's book, and presents them in a most exquisite format. The DVD can be ordered at relaxintosex.com.

Hicks, Esther and Jerry. *Introducing Abraham: The Secret Behind "The Secret."* Carlsbad, CA: Hay House, 2007.

This is one of the very finest DVDs we've ever seen on anything to do with spirituality. Prepare to have your mind blown as you meet the non-physical entity Abraham, alternately described as "infinite intelligence" and "the purest form of love ever encountered." This DVD—produced and hosted by Peter—is the perfect introduction to Esther and Jerry Hicks, and Abraham.

Richardson, Diana. *The Heart of Tantric Sex: A Unique Guide to Love and Sexual Fulfillment.* Mantra Books, 2003.

Diana's work provided the initial spark for us, and this particular book is the direct inspiration for the present volume. Diana reveals how the ancient practice of Tantra, with its unique, intelligent approach to sex, enhances intimacy and deepens love. Her website is www.loveforcouples.com.

Richardson, Diana and Michael. *Tantric Sex for Men: Making Love a Meditation.* Rochester, VT: Destiny Books, 2010.

From Amazon: "This book includes tried-and-true foreplay approaches and diagrams of sexual position sequences. It covers ways to increase sexual sensitivity through awareness, and how to have ecstatic experiences through reaching a woman's body on a sexually deeper level."

Richardson, Diana. *Tantric Orgasm for Women.* Rochester, VT: Destiny Books, 2004.

From Amazon: "Exploring Tantra from the female perspective, Diana Richardson reveals the critical role of receptive feminine energy. Her twenty years of Tantric research provide an understanding of how women can exert a powerful influence on their sexual experiences when they understand the inner workings of their bodies and avoid adopting conventional ideas about what should be satisfying to them."

Richardson, Diana. *Slow Sex: The Path to Fulfilling and Sustainable Sexuality.* Rochester, VT: Destiny Books, 2011.

From Amazon: "Exploring the healing, spiritual power of slow sex, this book offers a step-by-step guide for committed couples to transform sex into a meditative, loving union of complementary energies. It explains how slow sex increases sensitivity and sexual vitality and how, because it creates and restores love, slow sex is loving sex. With a focus on coolness rather than heat, this practice provides couples a way to reach a shared meditative state and use it as a vehicle to achieve higher consciousness. Illustrating different positions for eye contact, deep sustained penetration, and soft penetration, this book reveals that sex truly can be sustainable and enjoyable well into old age."

Gibran, Khalil. *The Prophet.* New York: Alfred A. Knopf, 1923.

From Amazon: "A collection of poetic essays that are philosophical, spiritual, and, above all, inspirational. Gibran's musings are divided into twenty-eight chapters covering such sprawling topics as love, marriage, children, giving, eating and drinking, work, joy and sorrow, housing, clothes, buying and selling, crime and punishment, laws, freedom, reason and passion, pain, self-knowledge, teaching, friendship, talking, time, good and evil, prayer, pleasure, beauty, religion, and death."

Osho. *Creativity: Unleashing the Forces Within.* New York: St. Martin's Griffin, 1999.

Peter has been powerfully influenced by the works of Osho. This is his very favorite Osho book, the one he often gives to friends.

From Amazon: "*Creativity* is a handbook for those who understand the need to bring more creativity, playfulness, and flexibility into their lives. It's a manual for thinking outside the box—and learning to live there as well."

Osho. *Tantra: The Supreme Understanding.* New York: St. Martin's Griffin, 2009.

From Amazon: "Osho discusses the mystical insights found in the ancient Tantric writings, and the many significant Tantric meditation techniques that are as relevant to the modern-day seeker as they were to those in earlier times. As always, Osho brings his own unique blend of wisdom, humor, and thought-provoking inspiration to even this complex subject, making it accessible to the widest possible audience."

Osho. *Love, Freedom, Aloneness: The Koan of Relationships.* New York: St. Martin's Griffin, 2002.

From Amazon: "Osho explains that in our post-ideological world, where old moralities are out of date, we have a golden opportunity to redefine and revitalize the very foundations of our lives. We have the chance to start afresh with ourselves and our relationships to others, and to find fulfillment and success for the individual and for society as a whole."

Osho. *Meditation: The First and Last Freedom.* New York: St. Martin's Griffin, 2004.

From Amazon: "Contains practical, step-by-step guides to a wide variety of meditation techniques selected by and/ or created by Osho, including the unique OSHO Active Meditations, which deal with the special tensions of contemporary life. Recognizing that it's almost impossible for most people these days just to stop and sit silently, these meditations—including the Osho Dynamic Meditation and Osho Kundalini Meditation—begin with one or more stages of vigorous physical activity. This brings our physical and mental energies to a peak, so that the following silence is easy—leaving us alert, refreshed, and newly energized."

Osho. *Sex Matters: From Sex to Superconciousness*. New York: St. Martin's Griffin, 2003.

From Amazon: "The Osho approach to sex begins with an understanding of how important love is in our lives, while at the same time acknowledges that the journey into love cannot exclude our innate biological energies. With this perspective, it becomes clear that the tendency for religions, and for society in general, to associate sex with sin and morality has been a great misfortune. Osho proposes a vision that embraces sex as a fundamental gift from nature. We learn how orgasm offers a glimpse of timelessness, thoughtlessness, and pure awareness—biology's way of pointing toward the consciousness that helps us to understand ourselves."

Osho. *Being in Love: How to Love with Awareness and Relate Without Fears*. New York: St. Martin's Griffin, 2008.

From Amazon: "In this thoughtful, provocative work, Osho—one of the most revolutionary thinkers of our time— challenges us to question what we think we know about love and opens us to the possibility of a love that is natural, fulfilling, and free of possessiveness and jealousy. With his characteristic wit, humor, and understanding, Osho dares us to resist the unhealthy relationship patterns we've learned from those around us, and to rediscover the meaning of love for ourselves."

Osho. *Intimacy: Trusting Oneself and the Other*. New York: St. Martin's Griffin, 2001.

From Amazon: "In this gentle and compassionate guide, Osho takes his readers step-by-step through what makes people afraid of intimacy, how to encounter those fears and go beyond them, and what they can do to nourish themselves and their relationships to support more openness and trust."

Osho. *Joy: The Happiness That Comes from Within*. New York: St. Martin's Griffin, 2009.

From Amazon: "Osho shows us that joy is the essence of life, that even unhappiness has its root in joy. He encourages us to accept joy by being grateful to be alive and for the challenges and opportunities in life, and by finding the good in all that we have—rather than setting conditions or demands for happiness. By embracing joy, one comes closer to a true, peaceful, and balanced state."

Hicks, Esther and Jerry. *Ask and It Is Given: Learning to Manifest Your Desires*. Carlsbad, CA: Hay House, 2004.

We have been powerfully influenced by, and have immense appreciation for, the message of Abraham-Hicks. This is their first major book, and the keys to the kingdom are contained within.

Hicks, Esther and Jerry. *The Law of Attraction: The Basics of the Teachings of Abraham.* Carlsbad, CA: Hay House, 2006.

From Amazon: "The understanding that you'll achieve by reading this book will take all the guesswork out of daily living. You'll finally understand just about everything that's happening in your own life as well as in the lives of those you're interacting with. This book will help you to joyously be, do, or have anything that you desire."

Hicks, Esther and Jerry. *The Vortex: Where the Law of Attraction Assembles all Cooperative Relationships.* Carlsbad, CA: Hay House, 2009.

From Amazon: "This book uncovers a myriad of false premises that are at the heart of every uncomfortable relationship issue, and guides you to a clear understanding of the powerful creative Vortex that has already assembled the relationships that you have desired. Abraham will show you how to enter that Vortex, where you will rendezvous with everything and everyone you have been looking for."

Hicks, Esther and Jerry. *The Law of Attraction in Action.* DVD series. Carlsbad, CA: Hay House, 2008–2010.

This twelve-part DVD series features the very best of Abraham, taking questions from people from all over the world asking about every subject under the sun.

Hicks, Esther and Jerry. *Getting into the Vortex: Guided Meditations.* CD and User Guide. Carlsbad, CA: Hay House, 2010.

This unique recording contains four powerfully guided daily meditations that have been designed to get you into the Vortex of Creation in four basic areas of your life: general well-being, financial well-being, physical well-being, and relationships.

Roberts, Jane, and Robert F. Butts. *Seth Speaks: The Eternal Validity of the Soul.* San Rafael, CA: Amber-Allen Publishing, 1994.

From Amazon: "One of the most powerful of the Seth Books, this essential guide to conscious living clearly and powerfully articulates the furthest reaches of human potential, and the concept that we all create our own reality according to our individual beliefs. Having withstood the test of time, it is still considered one of the most dynamic and brilliant maps of inner reality available today."

Williamson, Marianne. *A Return to Love: Reflections on the Principles of "A Course in Miracles."* New York: Harper Paperbacks, 1990.

From Amazon: "Williamson reveals how we each can become a miracle worker by accepting God and by the expression of love in our daily lives. Whether psychic pain is in the area of relationships, career, or health, she shows us how love is a potent force, the key to inner peace, and how by practicing love we can make our own lives more fulfilling while creating a more peaceful and loving world for our children."

Deida, David. *It's a Guy Thing: An Owner's Manual for Women*. Deerfield Beach, FL: Health Communications, Inc., 1997.

From Amazon: "Based on questions from women who have attended author David Deida's highly acclaimed relationships seminars, this must-have book puts male behavior under the microscope. Included are chapters on sex, work, relationships, and communication. Interspersed throughout are sidebars that shed light on the many faces of men, and help women grasp what makes men act the way they do."

Deida, David. *The Way of the Superior Man: A Spiritual Guide to Mastering the Challenges of Women, Work, and Sexual Desire*. Boulder, CO: Sounds True, 2006.

From Amazon: "David Deida explores the most important issues in men's lives—from career and family to women and intimacy to love and spirituality—to offer a practical guidebook for living a masculine life of integrity, authenticity, and freedom."

Deida, David. *The Enlightened Sex Manual: Sexual Skills for the Superior Lover*. Boulder, CO: Sounds True, 2007.

From Amazon: "The secret to enlightenment and great sex is revealed to be one and the same in this groundbreaking manual for adventurous lovers. David Deida was trained for decades in the art of spiritual and sexual awakening. Now he presents the ultimate collection of skills for opening to the physical, emotional, and spiritual rewards of intimate embrace. This book teaches you how to transform simple "skin friction" into the depths and embodiment of ecstasy, how to develop sexual abilities as gifts of heart rapture and bodily surrender, how to achieve the principal types of orgasm—and all their varieties—and much more."

Walsch, Neale Donald. *Conversations with God, Books 1–3.* New York: Putnam, 1996.

Both Jody and Peter have been greatly influenced by the writings of Neale Donald Walsch. As mentioned in our foreword to this book, Jody has had some one-on-one discussions with Neale, and in Peter's case, he produced a DVD called *Introducing Neale Donald Walsch: God's Latest Scribe.*

From Amazon: "The first installment of an extraordinary trilogy, *Conversations with God* marks Neale Donald Walsch's initial dialogue with God. This book discusses personal issues such as prosperity, relationships, and the nature of spiritual truth—with God providing clear, understandable answers. You'll realize that your own understanding of and conversation with God is the true subject matter of this unforgettable text."

Walsch, Neale Donald. *Neale Donald Walsch on Relationships.* Charlottesville, VA: Hampton Roads Publishing, 1997.

From Amazon: "Neale examines the patterns that hinder our ability to build and maintain successful relationships, teaches us to move beyond restrictive ways of relating, and explores different types of relationships—with God, with self, with others—demonstrating how they all affect and enhance one another."

Fife, Bruce, and Jon Kabara. *The Coconut Oil Miracle.* New York: Avery Trade, 2002.

From Amazon: "Coconut oil really is a miracle. Besides its use as a sexual lubricant, this natural fruit extract is used to lose weight; prevent heart disease, cancer, and diabetes; and beautify skin and hair."

Copeland, Pala, and Al Link. *Soul Sex: Tantra for Two.* Franklin Lakes, NJ: New Page Books, 2003.

From Amazon: "Pala and Al offer their partnership as a model for a successful, long-term relationship that is happy, fulfilled, and spiritually awakened. *Soul Sex* includes thought-provoking discussions, personal anecdotes, and precise but simple techniques to inspire you to apply to your daily life. The observations and exercises included are drawn from the authors' own heady partnership and from the hundreds of couples they have had the privilege to teach at their Tantra sacred sex workshops."

Warren, Sharon. *Magnetizing Your Heart's Desire.* Fountain Hills, AZ: Amazing Grace Unlimited Press, 2005.

From Amazon: "Each book contains a unique set of rare-earth magnets to quickly demonstrate and understand "hands on" how you attract your heart's desires; how to consistently be a Deliberate Creator; empowering tools that create, activate, and magnetize more joy in every arena of your life (relationships, love, money, career, home)."

Goddard, Neville. *Awakened Imagination.* Marina del Rey, CA: DeVorss & Company, 1954.

From Amazon: "Using short quotations from the Bible and from Blake, Yeats, Emerson, Lawrence, Quintillian, Hermes, and the Hermetica, Neville reveals the Power that makes the achievement of aims and the attainment of desires."

Tolle, Eckhart. *The Power of Now: A Guide to Spiritual Enlightenment.* Novato, CA: New World Library, 2004.

From Amazon: "Eckhart Tolle uses simple language and an easy question-and-answer format to guide us. A word-of-mouth phenomenon since its first publication, *The Power of Now* is one of those rare books with the power to create an experience in readers, one that can radically change their lives for the better."

Belitz, Charlene, and Meg Lundstrom. *The Power of Flow: Practical Ways to Transform Your Life with Meaningful Coincidence.* New York: Three Rivers Press, 1998.

Based on groundbreaking research, *The Power of Flow* goes beyond other books on synchronicity to provide you with sixteen easy-to-understand techniques that allow you to access this magical state of flow and create a richer, more satisfying life.

To Write to the Authors

If you wish to contact the authors or would like more information about this book, please write to the authors in care of Llewellyn Worldwide Ltd. and we will forward your request. Both the authors and publisher appreciate hearing from you and learning of your enjoyment of this book and how it has helped you. Llewellyn Worldwide Ltd. cannot guarantee that every letter written to the authors can be answered, but all will be forwarded. Please write to:

Jody Baron and Peter Beamish
℅ Llewellyn Worldwide
2143 Wooddale Drive
Woodbury, MN 55125-2989

Please enclose a self-addressed stamped envelope for reply,
or $1.00 to cover costs. If outside the U.S.A., enclose
an international postal reply coupon.